GCSE Music
Edexcel Areas of Study

This book takes you through everything you need to know about the
Areas of Study for Edexcel's GCSE music course.

Every topic is broken down into simple, manageable chunks,
so you know exactly what you need to learn.

What CGP is all about

Our sole aim here at CGP is to produce the highest quality
books — carefully written, immaculately presented and
dangerously close to being funny.

Then we work our socks off to get them out to you
— at the cheapest possible prices.

Contents

SECTION FOUR — AoS3: POPULAR MUSIC IN CONTEXT

SECTION FIVE — AoS4: WORLD MUSIC

SECTION SIX — BONUS TRACK

SECTION SEVEN — GLOSSARY AND INDEX

Published by Coordination Group Publications Ltd.

Contributors:

John Deane, Elena Delaney, Heather Gregson, Peter Hooper, Bryony Jones, David Jones, Luke von Kotze,
Angela E. Major, Glenn Rogers, Caley Simpson, Faye Stringer and Jennifer Underwood

With thanks to Sam Norman and Nikki Ball for the proofreading.

Acknowledgements

Page 34, Electric Counterpoint, Steve Reich © Copyright Hendon Music Inc. Reproduced by permission of Boosey & Hawkes
Music Publishers Ltd.

Page 38, Something's Coming, Leonard Bernstein © Copyright 1959 by Amberson Holdings LLC and Stephen Sondheim.
Copyright renewed, Leonard Bernstein Music Publishing Company LLC.

Page 45, All Blues, Music by Miles Davis © Copyright 1959 Jazz Horn Music Corporation, USA Universal/MCA Music
Limited. Used by permission of Music Sales Limited. All Rights Reserved. International Copyright Secured.

Page 51, Why Does My Heart Feel So Bad? Words and Music by Richard Hall © 1999 The Little Idiot Music
Warner/Chappell North America, London W6 8BS. Reproduced by permission of Faber Music Ltd. All Rights Reserved.

Page 66, Koko © Sunset France Productions, www.playasound.com

Every effort has been made to locate copyright holders and obtain permission to reproduce sources.
For those sources where it has been difficult to trace the copyright holder of the work, we would be grateful
for information. If any copyright holder would like us to make an amendment to the acknowledgements,
please notify us and we will gladly update the book at the next reprint. Thank you.

With thanks to Laura Jakubowski for the copyright research.

ISBN: 978 1 84762 372 0

Groovy website: www.cgpbooks.co.uk
Jolly bits of clipart from CorelDRAW®
Printed by Elanders Hindson Ltd, Newcastle upon Tyne

Based on the classic CGP style created by Richard Parsons

What You Have to Do for GCSE Music

Music GCSE doesn't cover every single aspect of music — if it did it would take forever. Instead you focus on four main 'Areas of Study' (AoS for short).

You learn about Four Areas of Study

For each Area of Study you'll learn the basics of that style or period — e.g. the musical structures, the instruments used, the context the music was originally created in, etc. You'll also have to give your opinions on music — using appropriate musical terms.
You have to look at set pieces for each Area of Study:

> **AoS1 — WESTERN CLASSICAL MUSIC, 1600-1899 (covered in Section 2)**
> Your set pieces are Handel's chorus *And The Glory of The Lord* from 'Messiah', the 1st Movement from Mozart's *Symphony No. 40 in G minor*, and Chopin's *Prelude No. 15 in D flat major*.

> **AoS2 — MUSIC IN THE TWENTIETH CENTURY (covered in Section 3)**
> Your set pieces are Schoenberg's *Peripetie* from 'Five Orchestral Pieces', *Something's Coming* from Bernstein's 'West Side Story', and the 3rd Movement from *Electric Counterpoint* by Reich.

> **AoS3 — POPULAR MUSIC IN CONTEXT (covered in Section 4)**
> Your set pieces are Miles Davis's *All Blues* from the album 'Kind of Blue', *Grace* from the album 'Grace' by Jeff Buckley and Moby's *Why Does My Heart Feel So Bad?* from the album 'Play'.

> **AoS4 — WORLD MUSIC (covered in Section 5)**
> Your set pieces are *Chuir M'Athair Mise Dhan Taigh Charraideach (Skye Waulking Song)* by Capercaillie from the album 'Nàdurra', some examples of a Rag Desh (the examiners have suggested some pieces — see p. 63-64) and *Yiri* by Koko.

They test you with Coursework...

The coursework is work done during the course. Obviously. It's split into two chunks:

PERFORMING

worth 30% of the total marks

1) You do two performances.
2) One has to be a solo performance. This can be a piece you play or sing, an improvisation, a sequenced performance or a realisation (see p. 2).
3) The other has to be an ensemble piece. You can perform or direct the performance, or provide a multitrack recording.

COMPOSING

worth 30% of the total marks

1) You compose or arrange two pieces.
2) Each one is based on a different Area of Study.

...and a Listening Exam

worth 40% of the total marks

At the end of Year 11 you do an exam called Listening and Appraising. You listen to extracts from the set pieces from all four Areas of Study and answer questions on what you hear.

Err, Miss... is it too late to change to physics?

Welcome to the wonderful world of GCSE Music. Breathe in the cool clear air. Listen to the birds. It's so beautiful, I could cry. Well actually, I couldn't, but it's OK compared to some subjects.

Unit 1 — Performing Music

Pick your pieces carefully and practise till your fingers bleed and the neighbours beg for mercy.

You have to do Two Performances

SOLO PERFORMANCE

You simply play one solo piece of your own choice. It can be a traditional performance, an improvisation, a sequenced performance (see p. 48) or a realisation. A sequenced performance must have at least three independent parts on individual MIDI tracks. A realisation is a performance that can't be assessed using the same criteria as the others — like a DJ performance or music that's been passed down orally.

ENSEMBLE PERFORMANCE

1) If you're playing in the ensemble, then there must be at least two of you playing or singing, and your part can't be doubled by any other part.

2) If you're rehearsing and directing the ensemble then there must be at least three players, and you're not allowed to play in the ensemble yourself.

3) Like the solo performance, this can be a traditional performance or an improvisation. You can choose to sequence the piece instead, but the ensemble piece still has to include live performances that you've recorded as part of a multitrack recording.

4) Talk to your teacher if you're going to use music technology, to make sure you get it right.

You have 10 hours to complete each recording (which should be no longer than 5 minutes), and your teacher has to be there. If you direct a piece, you have to hand in a DVD showing the performance and 2-5 minutes of rehearsal time. For both performances, you have to hand in a score, professional recording or commentary of your piece, or for an improvisation, the stimulus used (e.g. the chord pattern you used). You can do each performance on a different instrument if you want.

You get marks for the Quality of your Playing...

In each performance, you need to show off your 'musicality'. You get marks for:

1) *ACCURACY* This is the easiest bit. Learn the notes, play them in time and in tune. Most importantly, keep going — lots of stopping and starting or slowing down for tricky bits will lose you marks. Don't worry about the odd slip because of nerves, but start off well prepared.

2) *INTERPRETATION* Your performance needs to be expressive — to make the audience feel something. Pay attention to stuff like dynamics, tempo, mood, articulation and phrasing. If they're not written in, work out your own. Use expression and playing techniques that fit the style of your piece — e.g. don't play a lullaby on a distorted electric guitar.

3) *ENSEMBLE SKILLS* Obviously you only get marks for this when you're playing in an ensemble. Play in time and in tune with the other players. Really listen to the other parts, so you know when you should be part of the background and when you should make your part stand out.

...and marks for the Difficulty of the Piece

It's obvious really — a very simple piece will get fewer marks for difficulty than a complicated piece. But there's no point trying to play something that you're not capable of and then messing it up...

CHOOSE YOUR PIECES CAREFULLY

1) Ideally they should be the hardest level that you can play well.
2) If you pick something too easy, you'll be throwing away difficulty marks.
3) If you pick something too hard, you won't be able to play your best, and you'll lose marks for musicality.
4) Get your music teacher or instrument teacher's advice on what to play.

Practice makes perfect...

No doubt people have been going on at you about practising since you were knee-high to a piccolo. The more my music teachers went on at me about practising, the less I felt like doing it. I expect you know that you need to do lots of practice. So we'll just leave it there.

Unit 2 — Composing Music

When you write your GCSE pieces you don't just <u>fiddle about</u> until you've got a tune you like. You have to use the <u>Areas of Study</u> for ideas. You can also choose to <u>arrange</u> existing pieces instead...

You have to write Two Pieces for Coursework

1) You have to write <u>two</u> pieces. They can be for <u>one instrument</u> or <u>more</u> and you can use <u>acoustic</u> or <u>electronic</u> instruments. The total playing time for the two pieces should be between <u>2 and 4 minutes</u>.

2) You have to base both pieces on different <u>Areas of Study</u> — you can base your composition on any <u>style</u> or <u>form</u> within the AoS. So if Composition 1 is based on your study of music in the twentieth century (AoS2), you'd have to use something from AoS1, 3 or 4 for Composition 2.

3) You can do <u>arrangements</u> instead of compositions if you like — 2 compositions, 2 arrangements or one of each is allowed. Have a chat with your teacher if you're thinking about the arrangement option — to get <u>high marks</u>, your arrangement needs to be <u>noticeably different</u> to the existing piece. You basically have to create a <u>whole new piece</u> based on the original.

4) You can <u>perform</u> or <u>direct</u> (or <u>sequence</u>) one of your compositions as part of your performance assessment if you want.

5) You have <u>unlimited time</u> to do <u>research</u> on your compositions (and you can even do <u>rough drafts</u> in this time). You have <u>10 hours</u> to record and produce your final scores for <u>each</u> composition — this'll be <u>supervised</u> by your teacher.

It's marked on Six different Criteria

<u>Each</u> composition is worth <u>30 marks</u>. Both are marked on <u>three compulsory core criteria</u> and <u>three optional criteria</u>. The optional criteria are chosen from a list. Each criterion is worth <u>5 marks</u>. Your <u>teacher</u> or <u>examiner</u> will decide which optional criteria your pieces are marked on. They choose ones that are <u>appropriate</u> for your compositions (so they won't choose 'Use of Technology' if you haven't used any).

Core Criteria:	Optional Criteria:	
A) Use and development of ideas	D) Melody	G) Tempo/rhythm
B) Exploitation of the medium	E) Harmony/accompaniment	H) Dynamic contrasts
C) Structure and form.	F) Texture	I) Use of technology.

Arrangements are marked on different criteria:

Core Criteria:
A) Use and development of ideas
B) Exploitation of the medium
C) Choice of material/extent of change/impact.

Optional Criteria:
D) Melodic interest/part writing
E) Harmony/accompaniment
F) Texture
G) Tempo/rhythm
H) Dynamic contrasts
I) Use of technology
J) Technical problems.

You have to hand in a <u>recording</u> of each composition, as well as a <u>written version</u>. There's more information about these on the next page.

Unlimited time — I'd rather have unlimited cake...

The music you study for the four topics is meant to be more than just exam fodder — it's supposed to be an <u>inspiration</u>. So it's doubly important that you get <u>listening</u> and <u>learning</u> about it.

Unit 2 — Composing Music

Well, the good news is — the compositions you have to do for GCSE only need to be a total of between 2 and 4 minutes long. No one's expecting an opera. Something short will do.

To get Top Marks think about...

1) **USING YOUR RESOURCES TO FULL POTENTIAL**
   - Once you've chosen the instruments, think about all the ways they can make interesting and contrasting sounds — e.g. pizzicato bits for strings.
   - Remember the limitations — e.g. clarinet players need time to breathe.
   - Think about the highest and lowest notes your chosen instruments can play — there's no point composing a brilliant piece if no one can play it.

2) **STRUCTURE**
   Organise your music with a clear, definite structure — see p. 5 and Section 2 of this book and Section 5 of the Core Book for ideas. Even if your composition doesn't follow a traditional form, you'll need to make sure it doesn't just ramble on aimlessly.

3) **DEVELOPING YOUR MUSICAL IDEAS**
   Don't just use a good idea once and then forget about it. Build up and develop the good bits — e.g. by changing the rhythm from short notes to long notes or the key from major to minor. See Section 6 in the Core Book for loads more techniques and devices for developing your ideas.

4) **MAKING THE STYLE CONVINCING**
   Listen to lots of music from the style you're composing in. Make your piece sound like 'the real thing' by using similar musical ideas — e.g. in a reggae song use offbeat staccato quavers, syncopated bass lines and muted guitar.

5) **MAKING ARRANGEMENTS CREATIVE**
   In arrangements, you get marks for your creative ideas. Just rewriting an existing tune for new instruments won't get you a decent mark — you'll have to bring in new ideas of your own. Keep a copy of the piece you're working on — you have to hand it in with your finished arrangement.

Decide how to Hand In your work

For each piece, you give in two things — a written version and a recording (you've got 10 hours to do these for each composition — see p. 3). You've got a few options for how you present each one.

> **WRITTEN VERSION**
> This can be...
> - a score — either handwritten or computer generated.
>   It can be in any appropriate format, e.g. a full score, a lead sheet or chord chart.
> - a written commentary with detailed performance directions and a description of the composition process.
>
> Give as much information as possible. Details of dynamics, tempo, expression and articulation will all improve your mark. There should be enough detail for someone else to be able to more-or-less recreate your piece. If you do an arrangement, you need to hand in the original score as well.

> **RECORDING**
> 1) The recording can be on CD, MiniDisc or MP3.
> 2) You don't get any marks for recording quality, but good recordings are easier to mark.

I'm going to submit my work by telepathy...

On the one hand, you've got almost two years to get these compositions sorted. On the other hand, if you don't start ASAP you might just find yourself running out of time. Best get on with it.

How Music is Organised

When you're <u>composing</u> your pieces, it's a good plan to think about how you want to <u>organise</u> them.
If you just start composing without any <u>idea</u> of <u>where</u> the music's going, it'll probably end up in a bit of a <u>mess</u>.

Music needs Form and Structure

1) Music's got to be organised, or it just sounds like a load of <u>random notes</u>.
2) The <u>most basic</u> bit of organisation is the timing <u>(beats in a bar)</u>. The next biggest chunk is the <u>phrasing</u>.
3) The <u>overall shape</u> is called the <u>structure</u> or <u>form</u>.
4) The structure could be the <u>verses</u> and <u>chorus</u> in a pop song, or the <u>movements</u> of a symphony.
5) Composers usually <u>decide</u> on the <u>structure</u> of a piece of music <u>before</u> they get into the detail.
6) You have to base each composition on an <u>Area of Study</u>, so have a look through this book to see what <u>structures</u> you might want to use.

Most music uses Repetition Repetition Repetition ...

1) <u>Repetition</u> means using a <u>musical idea</u> — a chunk of tune — <u>more than once</u>.
2) Repeating bits is a really good way of giving music <u>shape</u>. Once the audience know a tune, it works like a <u>landmark</u> — they know where they are when they hear that tune <u>later</u> in the piece. That's how <u>choruses</u> work.
3) If you're planning <u>your own</u> piece of music, try repeating the best part of the tune.
4) You can even repeat <u>whole sections</u> — e.g. in <u>rondo form</u> (see p. 9), the main theme is repeated lots of times.

Rhubarb, rhubarb, rhubarb, rhubarb, rhubarb...

Ousland.

...and Contrast

1) Repetition is really important — but <u>constant repetition</u> is <u>boring</u>.
2) Good compositions balance repetition with <u>contrast</u>. The aim is to do something <u>different</u> from the repeated bits to add <u>variety</u>.
3) There's contrast in just about <u>every</u> piece of music — have a look at p. 6 for some ways of using contrast in your compositions.
4) The <u>verse and chorus structure</u> of a pop song is one of the most obvious ways of using contrast — the different <u>sections</u> contrast with each other.
5) In <u>rondo form</u>, different sections contrast with the <u>repeated section</u>.

When you're composing, make plans Before you start

1) Making a <u>musical plan</u> helps to <u>organise</u> your ideas — it's a bit like writing an essay plan.
2) It's OK to <u>design your own</u> musical plan, but a lot of people use '<u>tried and tested</u>' structures like the ones described in Section Two — because they know they'll work.
3) 'Tried and tested' structures are like <u>templates</u>. The <u>general organisation</u> of your ideas is decided for you — you just need to add the <u>details</u>.
4) Your plan should include ways to <u>vary</u> the different <u>sections</u> — have a look on p. 6 for some ideas.

Best laid plans — will surely work out fine and dandy...

You know those <u>organised people</u> — the ones who remember all their friends' <u>birthdays</u>, never forget to feed the <u>goldfish</u> or walk their little sister back after swimming and always have <u>clean matching socks</u> on? Well, we can't all be like that, but at least we can try and keep our <u>music</u> organised. It's some consolation.

Contrast

A balanced diet of <u>repetition</u> and <u>contrast</u> is what every musical structure needs to stay in tip-top condition. Here's the lowdown on musical contrast — use these ideas in <u>your compositions</u>.

There are Lots of Ways to Create Contrast

Bringing in a <u>new tune</u> is the <u>simplest</u> way to make one chunk of music contrast with another.
If you change <u>other things</u> about the music, as well as the tune, you get <u>more noticeable</u> contrasts...

1) Use Different Keys to alter the mood

1) The key a tune is written in gives it a definite <u>character</u> or <u>mood</u>.
2) Changing key midway through a piece is a good way to create a contrasting mood — it's called <u>modulation</u>.
3) Pieces usually modulate to a <u>related key</u> like the <u>dominant</u> or <u>relative minor</u>.

See Section Four in the Core Book for more on <u>modulation</u>.

You could have a piece that opens in C major... → **C MAJOR** bright, happy mood   ...then modulates to the <u>relative minor</u>. → **A MINOR** sad mood

2) Change Short Jumpy notes for Long Smooth notes

You can change the <u>rhythm</u> and <u>articulation</u> to get a big change in mood.

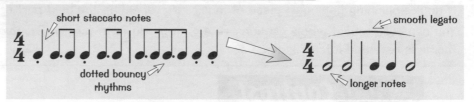

short staccato notes
dotted bouncy rhythms
smooth legato
longer notes

3) Switch from Loud to Soft or Fast to Slow

<u>Dynamic changes</u> and <u>tempo changes</u> are probably the easiest ways to change the feel of a tune — you get pretty much <u>instant results</u>.

This bit could be dramatic car-chase music.

LOUD — fortissimo (ff)
FAST — presto

→

SOFT — pianissimo (pp)
SLOW — largo

Sombre-sounding funeral music — maybe the good guy's girlfriend just died.

4) Change the Texture — go from a Thin Sound to a Full Sound

Changing <u>texture</u> is another great way to make musical contrast.
On a piano, a section with just one line of tune with a <u>thin</u>, <u>weedy sound</u> would contrast starkly with one where the tune's accompanied by <u>hefty chords</u>.

SECTION A — The pianist plays a tune with the right hand only.

SECTION B — The pianist plays the same tune with rich left-hand chords.

See Section Four of the Core Book for more on <u>texture</u>.

You can do it by varying the number of instruments too — go from a <u>lush rich orchestration</u> to an <u>instrument playing alone</u>.

Green tights and red shoes — that's what I call contrast...

<u>Mix and match</u> ideas to put contrast into your pieces, but don't use them all at the same time or you'll end up with a crazy-sounding piece with <u>too much</u> contrast. Try changing just a few ideas at a time.

Listening Exam

When the coursework's done and handed in, you can just sit back and relax, can't you...
<u>NO YOU CAN'T</u> — you've got to do a <u>listening exam</u>. All <u>90 minutes</u> of it. Whoop-dee-doodle-DOO.

The Listening Exam tests all four Areas of Study

1) The Listening Exam is worth <u>40%</u> of your total mark — that's a big chunk of marks. The invigilator <u>plays music</u> from a CD. You listen to the music and answer <u>written questions</u> about it. It's divided into <u>two</u> sections — <u>Section A</u> and <u>Section B</u>.

2) There are <u>8</u> questions in Section A — most of them only need <u>short answers</u>. You have an <u>hour and five minutes</u> for this bit. You're given <u>extracts</u> from the <u>set pieces</u> to listen to — <u>each piece</u> has its own set of questions. You'll be told <u>what</u> the piece is and <u>how many times</u> it'll be played. You're given <u>one minute</u>'s <u>reading</u> time before each question, and <u>three minutes</u> afterwards to finish <u>writing</u> your answers. Concentrate on answering just a <u>few</u> of the questions each time the music's played — it's less <u>confusing</u>.

3) Section B has <u>two</u> questions, but you only need to answer <u>one</u> of them. You have <u>25 minutes</u> for this bit. There'll be a couple of parts worth just one or two marks, then a question that needs a <u>longer answer</u> (worth about 10 marks). You'll be marked on the <u>quality</u> of your writing, as well as your <u>knowledge</u> of the piece. The pieces in Section B <u>aren't</u> played for you — you have to write about them from <u>memory</u>.

Some questions are Multiple Choice

Don't make a botch by <u>rushing</u> these — read all the options <u>carefully</u>.

In which century was this piece composed?
Put a cross in the correct box.
☐ 16th   ☐ 17th   ☐ 18th   ☐ 19th

If you're stuck — <u>guess</u> the answer.
There's a <u>25% chance</u> of getting it right.

Some questions just need a Short Answer

These questions test your <u>detailed knowledge</u> of the AoS. They're only worth a few marks so don't waste time writing your answer out in a nice long sentence — just write down <u>one good word</u> for <u>each mark</u>.

Name two instruments playing the theme in this extract.
(2 marks)

Sometimes they give you an Outline of the music

You could get an <u>outline</u> of part of the music called a 'skeleton score'. It will just show <u>part</u> of the music — the melody, rhythm or lyrics, say. The skeleton score will help you with answering the question. You might be asked to <u>fill in</u> the pitch, rhythm or chords of a short section of the music.

Fill in the missing notes in bar 4.
The rhythm is given above the stave.

Questions in Section B need a Longer Answer

These are questions where you have to write a <u>longer</u> answer — a few <u>paragraphs</u> of continuous writing. Make sure you cover all the <u>key points</u> of the question in your answer — don't be afraid to mention the <u>obvious</u>.

Comment on how Leonard Bernstein uses the following musical elements in *Something's Coming*. Melody, harmony, tempo, rhythm, dynamics. *(10 marks)*

Shiver me timbers — 'tis the skeleton score...

If you think of an answer <u>while the CD's playing</u>, just use a <u>pencil</u> and scribble it down. The music <u>stops</u> to give you writing time after each question — use that time to write the answer neatly in pen.

Baroque and Classical Music

Baroque and Classical music are similar but not the same. Here's a rough guide to both types...

Baroque composers Used Major and Minor Scales

Baroque
1600–1750

1) From about 1600 Western composers stopped writing modal music.
2) Instead they used major and minor keys to write tonal music. This was a big change. In Western countries like the UK most music is still tonal, hundreds of years later.
3) Modulating (switching between related keys, see Section Four in the Core Book) turned out to be a good way of creating contrast in music.
4) Composers developed new structures for organising music using modulation and contrast, e.g. binary, ternary, rondo and variation forms (see p. 9).

Baroque has a Recognisable Sound

Baroque music's pretty easy to recognise. These are the main things to listen out for:

1) The dynamics change suddenly. Each bit is either loud or soft. You won't hear any gradual changes in volume — no crescendos or diminuendos. They're called terraced or stepped dynamics.
2) The melody's built up from short musical ideas (posh name = motifs), so you get a fair bit of repetition.
3) The harmonies are simple. They mainly use chords I and V (covered in Section Four in the Core Book).
4) The melody's swarming with ornaments added in to make it more interesting (see p. 12).
5) The texture's often contrapuntal (or polyphonic — see Section Four of the Core Book).

Most Baroque music had a Basso Continuo

1) A basso continuo is a continuous bass part. It's played throughout a piece, and the chords are based on it.
2) It was often played on an organ or harpsichord (harpsichords were popular Baroque instruments). It could also be played by more than one instrument — e.g. cellos, double basses and bassoons.
3) Other Baroque instruments are the flute, recorder, oboe, bassoon, and orchestral strings (violins, violas, cellos and double basses). See Section 7 in the Core Book for more on this.

Baroque turned into Classical Music

Classical music grew out of Baroque, so it's similar but not the same.

1) Classical music contains fewer ornaments than Baroque, and the pieces are very balanced. They tend to have equal four-bar phrases, split into a two-bar question and a two-bar answer.
2) Classical composers still wrote in binary, ternary, rondo and variation forms, but they also came up with a new structure called sonata form (see p. 19).
3) The dynamics are more subtle, using crescendos and diminuendos, not just changing suddenly.

Classical
1750–1820

New Instruments and Groups changed the sound

1) The piano was invented in about 1700. It got to be way more popular than the harpsichord because you could vary the dynamics. Classical composers went wild for the piano.
2) The clarinet was invented around this time too.
3) Orchestras got bigger — woodwind, trumpets and horns were used more and the string section expanded (see p. 16 for more about the Classical orchestra).

Baroque and ba-roll was invented later...

Make sure you know the key features of Baroque and Classical music — and the differences between them. The examiners might ask you to explain why your set piece is typical of the period it was written in.

Baroque and Classical Structures

On these two pages I've kindly *(gosh, I'm so kind)* stuck the structures most often used by Baroque and Classical composers to give their melodies a <u>shape</u>. *And I've ironed your shirt and pants.*

Music in Binary form has Two Sections

1) <u>Binary</u> means something like '<u>in two parts</u>' — there are <u>two bits</u> to a tune in <u>binary form</u>.

2) Binary form's usually used for <u>Baroque dances</u>, e.g. bourrée, menuet, gavotte, sarabande and gigue.

3) Each section is <u>repeated</u>. You play Section A twice, and then Section B twice — so you end up with <u>AABB</u>.

4) Section B <u>contrasts</u> with Section A — the two bits should sound <u>different</u>.

5) The contrast's often made by <u>modulating</u> to related keys. Pieces in a <u>minor</u> key usually modulate to the <u>relative major</u>, e.g. A minor to C major. Pieces in a <u>major</u> key usually modulate to the <u>dominant</u> key (V), e.g. C major to G major.

Ternary form has Three Sections

1) <u>Ternary</u> means '<u>in three parts</u>' — there are <u>three sections</u> in music with ternary form. Each section <u>repeats</u>, so it goes AABBAA.

2) Section A ends in the <u>home key</u>, normally with a <u>perfect cadence</u> (see Section Four in the Core Book). This makes it sound like a <u>complete piece</u> in itself.

3) In Section B the music modulates to a <u>related key</u>, like the dominant or relative minor, and then <u>goes back</u> to the home key before it ends.

4) The last section can be <u>exactly the same</u> as Section A, or a slightly <u>varied</u> version. If it <u>is</u> varied, you call it <u>A1</u> instead of A.

Baroque Composers used ternary form in Arias

An <u>aria</u> is a solo in an <u>opera</u> or <u>oratorio</u> (big vocal works — see p. 13). Arias in the <u>Baroque period</u> (1600-1750) are often in ternary form. This type of aria's often called a 'da capo aria'. <u>Handel</u> wrote lots of these.

After repeating Section A and Section B you come to the instruction <u>da capo al fine</u>. It means "go back to the beginning and play to the end". To tell you where the end is it says <u>fine</u> at the end of Section A.

Classical Composers used ternary form in Symphonies

1) In a Classical symphony (see p. 18-19), the <u>third movement</u>'s often in a ternary form called <u>minuet and trio</u>.
2) The trio's in a different (but related) key <u>for contrast</u>.
3) They're sandwiched together to give the <u>whole movement</u> a ternary structure.

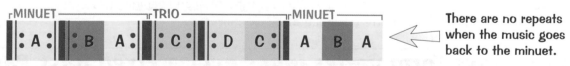

There are no repeats when the music goes back to the minuet.

Rondo Form can have Any Number of sections

1) <u>Rondo</u> means <u>going round</u>. A rondo starts with a main idea in <u>Section A</u>, moves into a <u>new section</u>, goes round again to <u>A</u>, moves into another <u>new section</u>, goes round again to <u>A</u>... as many times as you like. The <u>new section</u> after each Section A always <u>contrasts</u> with A.

2) Section A is known as the <u>main theme</u> or <u>refrain</u>. The contrasting sections are called <u>episodes</u>.

3) The main theme is always in the <u>home key</u>. Each <u>episode</u> tends to modulate to a <u>related key</u> for contrast.

Baroque and Classical Structures

Variations are pieces which start with one pattern or tune, and then change it in different ways. There are two main structures for variation. In the Baroque and Classical periods composers loved 'em better than their own babies. They're called 'theme and variation' and 'ground bass'.

Theme and Variation Form varies the melody

1) In theme and variation form, the theme's usually a memorable tune.

2) The theme's played first. There's a short pause before the first variation's played, then another pause before the next variation. Each variation is a self-contained piece of music. There can be as many or as few variations as the composer wants.

3) Each variation should be a recognisable version of the main theme, but different from all the others.

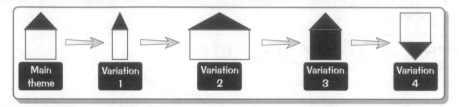

Main theme → Variation 1 → Variation 2 → Variation 3 → Variation 4

You can vary a tune in loads of simple ways:

1) Start off with a basic theme...

2) Add notes to make the tune more complex.

Posh name = ornamentation

3) Remove notes to simplify the tune.

4) Change the metre — say, from two beats in a bar to three.

5) Add a countermelody — an extra melody over the top of the theme.

6) You can also change the tempo, change the key (from major to minor or vice versa), change some or all of the chords or add a different type of accompaniment, e.g. a Classical 'Alberti bass' pattern instead of block chords.

Ground Bass Form varies ideas over a Fixed Bass Part

Ground bass is a continuous set of variations — there are no pauses. The main theme — called the ground — is a bass line which repeats throughout the piece. Varying melodies and harmonies which become gradually more complex are played over the ground. There are two types of baroque dance that are in ground bass form — the chaconne and passacaglia. They're quite slow and stately.

Freshly ground bass — it goes all powdery...

Neither of these structures is horrifically complicated — but it's easy to get one muddled up with another. These are good pages to learn painstakingly, tediously thoroughly so you can be sure you know what's what.

Baroque and Classical Melody Patterns

These are some of the more <u>sophisticated</u> ways Baroque and Classical composers developed their melodies.

Melodic Inversion — turning the tune Upside Down

1) <u>Melodic inversion</u> makes a melody sound very different, but not totally different.
2) You keep the <u>same intervals</u> between the notes, but they go in the <u>opposite direction</u>, i.e. down instead of up, and up instead of down. Basically you turn the tune on its head.

The first melody goes <u>up a major third</u> from C to E, then up a minor third to G.

In the inversion the melody goes <u>down a major third</u> to A♭, then down a minor third from A♭ to F.

Retrograde — playing the tune Backwards

Playing the notes <u>in reverse order</u> is called <u>retrograde</u>.

If you switch the notes so they're in reverse order <u>and</u> inverted, you get a <u>retrograde inversion</u>.

Sequencing — repeat a Pattern, vary the Pitch

1) Repeat the <u>pattern</u> of a phrase but start on a <u>different note</u>, higher or lower. This is called a <u>sequence</u>.
2) <u>Ascending</u> sequences go up in pitch. <u>Descending</u> sequences go down.
3) <u>Handel</u> used a <u>descending sequence</u> in bars 18-19 of *And the Glory of the Lord*.

Imitation — repeat a phrase with Slight Changes

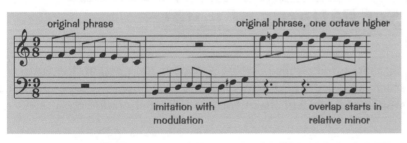

1) In <u>imitation</u> a phrase is repeated with <u>slight changes</u> each time.
2) It works really well if one instrument or voice imitates <u>another</u> and then <u>overlaps</u>.
3) Listen out for the imitation between the <u>alto</u> and <u>tenor</u> parts in Handel's *And the Glory of the Lord* (e.g. bars 63-68) and between the <u>clarinet</u> and <u>bassoon</u> in Mozart's *Symphony No. 40 in G Minor* (e.g. bars 72-76).

Ostinato — keep One Pattern the Same, Change the rest

1) This is called ostinato. One pattern's played <u>over and over</u> again.
2) The rest of the piece <u>changes round it</u>.
3) The ostinato doesn't have to be in the <u>bass</u> line — it can be in the <u>melody</u> or the <u>chord pattern</u>. It can last for more than one bar.

Here's the repeating pattern

Baroque and Classical Melody Patterns

Another way of livening up a melody that was VERY POPULAR with Baroque composers was adding in ornaments. Ornaments are fiddly little notes that stand out a bit from the main tune.

A Trill is lots of Tiny Quick Notes

1) In Baroque music the trill usually starts one note above the written note then goes quickly back and forth between the written note and the note you started on.

2) In Classical music the trill usually starts on the written note and goes up to the note above.

3) The second-last note is usually the one below the written note.

4) A sharp, flat or natural sign above the trill symbol tells you if the note to trill to is sharp, flat or natural.

5) Listen out for the trills in Mozart's *Symphony No. 40 in G Minor*.

HERE'S HOW YOU PLAY A TRILL IN CLASSICAL MUSIC

The trill lasts the same length of time as the written note.

Appoggiaturas Clash with the chord

1) An appoggiatura clashes with the accompanying chord.

2) It's written as a little note, and takes half the value of the following note.

3) The note before it is usually quite a jump away.

4) The note after the appoggiatura is always just above or below. It's called the resolution. The resolution has to be from the accompanying chord.

5) Appoggiaturas usually fall on a strong beat, so the resolution note falls on a weaker beat.

6) Appoggiaturas are also called grace notes. Another type of grace note is the acciaccatura, which looks a bit like an appoggiatura but has a line through it. Acciaccaturas are played very quickly.

diatonic appoggiatura   resolution   chromatic appoggiatura   resolution

Passing Notes link the notes Before and After

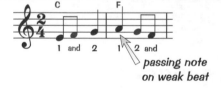

passing note on weak beat

1) The notes before and after a passing note have to belong to the accompanying chord.

2) They're usually put on weak beats. When they are on the strong beat they're called 'accented passing notes'.

Mordents and Turns are Set Patterns of notes

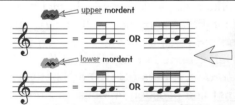

upper mordent

lower mordent

Mordents start off like trills. The difference is they end on the written note, which is played a bit longer than the trilled notes. There are loads of different mordents, but these two are the most common.

A turn starts on the note above the written note, then goes to the written note, followed by the note below the written note. It ends back on the written note.

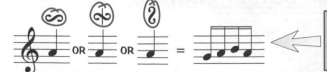

OR   OR

An inverted turn starts on the note below the written note, then goes through the written note, then the note above that, and finally back to the written note.

I've done my bit — now it's your turn...

All the stuff on these pages about Baroque and Classical music tells you how they put the melody line together. If you want to find out more about writing harmonies, have a squizz at Section 4 in the Core Content book.

Baroque Choral Music

Baroque composers wrote a lot of <u>choral music</u> — some of it's still performed <u>today</u>.

Choral Music is sung by Choirs and Soloists

Choral music can be <u>sacred</u> (religious) or <u>secular</u> (non-religious).

SACRED MUSIC

MASS	Part of the Catholic church service set to music.
REQUIEM	Mass for the dead.
CHORALE	A hymn.
ORATORIO	Religious version of an opera, often telling Bible stories.
CANTATA	Vocal pieces made up of two or three arias, separated by recitatives (see below).

SECULAR MUSIC

OPERA	A story set to music with singing and acting. Most operas were divided up into three parts (or 'Acts') The main types of Baroque opera were:
	Opera Seria (serious, often mythological themes),
	Opera Buffa (lighter, more everyday themes),
	Opéra Comique (like Opera Buffa, but with some spoken recitatives),
	Operetta (not big enough to be a proper opera).
CANTATA	You can get secular cantatas as well.

Operas, Oratorios and Cantatas have 3 Main Types of song

1) ARIA

An <u>aria</u> is a <u>solo vocal piece</u> (backed by the <u>orchestra</u>). It gives the <u>main characters</u> the chance to show what they're <u>thinking</u> and <u>feeling</u>. In England and France, they were sometimes called '<u>airs</u>' instead.

2) RECITATIVE

A <u>recitative</u> is a song which <u>tells the story</u> and <u>moves it along</u>. The rhythm of the words tends to imitate the <u>rhythm</u> of normal speech.

3) CHORUS

A <u>chorus</u> is sung by the <u>chorus</u> (a <u>choir</u>). Choruses are usually written for <u>SATB</u> choirs (Sopranos, Altos, Tenors and Basses). Most Baroque choirs were <u>all male</u> — the highest parts would be sung by <u>boy sopranos</u> (also called <u>trebles</u>).

Oratorios are Religious versions of Operas

1) Oratorios often tell <u>Bible stories</u>, or tales with a <u>religious</u> or <u>moral</u> theme.
2) They're <u>not</u> usually <u>acted out</u> with <u>scenery</u> and <u>costumes</u> (like operas are).
3) They normally have an <u>instrumental accompaniment</u>.
4) They can be performed in <u>concert halls</u> as well as <u>churches</u>.

Operas, Oratorios — there's Masses of stuff on this page...

Make sure you know the <u>difference</u> between <u>sacred</u> and <u>secular</u> music — and can give examples of each type. Being able to <u>describe</u> the different <u>types</u> of songs in operas, oratorios and cantatas will be useful too.

Handel — And the Glory of the Lord (Messiah)

Now it's time to get a handle on Handel, and meet the piece you have to study — *And the Glory of the Lord* from his oratorio 'Messiah'.

Handel was a German Composer

1) George Frideric Handel was born in Germany in 1685. From about 1710, he lived in England. He died in London in 1759 and is buried in Westminster Abbey.
2) He was popular with Queen Anne, George I and George II — he composed 'Zadok the Priest' for the coronation of George II, and it's been played at every coronation since then. He also wrote music for the Calvinist church in Germany and the Church of England.
3) Handel wrote loads of music, including lots of oratorios and operas (see p. 13). As well as choral music, he also wrote many orchestral pieces — one of the most famous is the 'Water Music'.

'Messiah' is a famous Oratorio

1) Handel wrote 'Messiah' in 1741. It only took him about 3 weeks to compose it (though he did pinch a few bits from his earlier compositions).
2) It became really popular with audiences because of its uplifting choruses — like the *Hallelujah Chorus*.
3) It was also very popular with other composers — Mozart liked it so much he arranged his own version of it.
4) 'Messiah' was originally supposed to be performed at Easter, but now it's usually sung at Christmas.
5) The libretto (text) was put together by Charles Jennens, who took words from the Old and New Testaments. Most of the words are from the King James Bible.
6) It was written for SATB choir, SATB soloists and a full Baroque orchestra. Handel wrote parts for oboes, bassoon, trumpets, timpani, strings and basso continuo — often a harpsichord (see p. 8). Mozart's later arrangement added flutes, clarinets, French horns, trombones and organ.

It's divided up into Three Parts

1) Like an opera, 'Messiah' is divided into three sections:
   - The first section describes the prophecies about Jesus' birth.
   - The middle section is about the persecution and crucifixion of Jesus.
   - The last section is about his resurrection.
2) Within each section, there are lots of different pieces — there's a mix of arias, recitatives and choruses (see p. 13). There's also a duet and some instrumental sections. There are arias and recitatives for soprano, alto, tenor and bass soloists. The famous *Hallelujah Chorus* is at the end of the second section.

You have to study a Chorus from 'Messiah'

1) The chorus you have to study, *And the Glory of the Lord*, is the fourth piece in the first section of 'Messiah'.
2) It comes after an aria sung by a tenor, and before a bass recitative.
3) It's the first chorus you hear in the oratorio.
4) The chorus is made up of the lines 'And the glory of the Lord shall be revealed', 'And all flesh shall see it together' and 'for the mouth of the Lord hath spoken it'. These phrases are repeated throughout the piece (the first is broken up into two parts — 'And the glory of the Lord' and 'shall be revealed', so there are actually four separate phrases).
5) For most of this chorus, the orchestra doubles the vocal parts — instruments often play in unison with the singers.

And the glory of GCSE Music shall be revealed...

Don't be fooled by some modern recordings of 'Messiah'. When it was first performed, it would have been sung by somewhere between 12 and 24 (all male) singers — not the hundreds you sometimes hear today.

Handel — And the Glory of the Lord (Messiah)

You need to know a bit more detail about *And the Glory of the Lord* — and be able to describe the key features. Have a listen to the piece and make sure you can spot all the bits mentioned on this page.

And the Glory of the Lord is in a Major Key

1) Most of *And the Glory of the Lord* is in A major, though it does modulate (change key) in a few places. It goes to E major twice, and B major once. It sounds happy and joyful.
2) The texture in most of the piece is homophonic (all the parts move together). Some bits are polyphonic (parts weaving in and out of each other). For example, in bars 91-107, all four vocal parts are singing different tunes at the same time.
3) The piece is marked *Allegro* — it's quick and lively. It's in 3/4, but in some places (e.g. bars 9-10), it feels like it's in 2/4 — this is called a hemiola.

There are Four main Musical Ideas

1) *And the Glory of the Lord* (like most of the choruses in 'Messiah') is made up of a few musical ideas (or motifs). Handel usually introduces these motifs very simply — just sung by one part, then weaves them into the rest of the music. The four motifs in this chorus go with the four phrases on p. 14.

(1)

1) The first motif is first sung by the altos in bars 11-14.
2) Most of this phrase is syllabic — each syllable has its own note.

(2)
1) The second motif's introduced by the tenors in bars 17-20.
2) The words 'be revealed' are spread over a descending sequence (see p.11).
3) The syllables of the word 'revealed' are spread over lots of notes — this is melismatic (the opposite of syllabic).

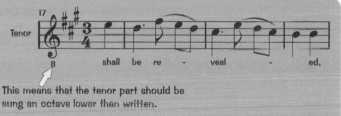

This means that the tenor part should be sung an octave lower than written.

(3)

1) The third motif is first sung by the altos in bars 43-46.
2) The same bit of melody is repeated three times.

(4)
1) The final motif is introduced by the tenors and basses in bars 51-57. It's the only motif that's introduced by two parts.
2) They sing in unison for the first 5 bars, then in harmony for the last two.
3) Most of the motif is on the same note (an A). This is a pedal point (or pedal note — a held-on note).
4) The notes are quite long (minims and dotted minims). It sounds serious and important.

2) Once the motifs have been introduced, the parts imitate each other (see p. 11) — for example, in bars 79-83, the altos and tenors begin a phrase, then the sopranos and basses start the same phrase (at a different pitch) one bar later. The parts overlap — they're singing in canon.
3) The last four bars of the piece are marked *Adagio* — they're much slower. It finishes with a plagal cadence (chord IV followed by chord I — see Section 4 of the Core Book). It makes the piece sound like it's finished.

Pedal as fast as you can...

Lots of religious pieces end with a plagal cadence — it's the 'Amen' cadence (i.e. when 'Amen' is sung at the end of a hymn, it'll be sung using notes from chord IV followed by chord I — a plagal cadence).

The Classical Orchestra

Moving swiftly on... After the joys of Baroque choral music, it's time to look at Classical music. Mozart's *Symphony No. 40 in G Minor* was written for an orchestra, so you need to know what a Classical orchestra was like.

Orchestral music was written for Wealthy Audiences

1) The Classical period began around 1750. At that time, composers worked for royalty and aristocrats. They were paid to write music for official events, church services and plain old entertainment. Composers had to write music that their patrons (employers) would approve of.

2) Later in the Classical period, society changed. Middle-class people had more money and wanted entertainment. Public concert halls were built, where people could go to listen to music.

3) Famous Classical composers like Haydn and Mozart worked for patrons, but they also put on concerts in the new concert halls. By the 1800s, composers could earn quite a bit of money from ticket sales at concert halls. This gave them more freedom — they could write for the tastes of concert-goers instead of just pleasing their patrons.

Orchestras Grew during the Classical Period

1) At the start of the Classical period, composers wrote for smallish orchestras — mainly strings, with horns, flutes and oboes. There'd be two horns and one or two woodwind.

2) Later on, the woodwind section grew — clarinets were invented during the Classical period, and were included in the orchestra. Mozart was the first composer to use the clarinet in a symphony (your set work has clarinets in it). Bassoons were introduced too.

3) Trumpets were added to the brass section, and timpani were included in the percussion section.

4) In some early Classical music, there'd be a harpsichord (see p. 8), but after a while composers stopped using it. The harpsichord was there to fill in the harmonies, but it wasn't really needed once the extra woodwind had been added.

5) This is a fairly typical layout for a later Classical orchestra:

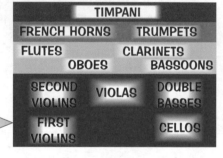

TIMPANI		
FRENCH HORNS		TRUMPETS
FLUTES		CLARINETS
OBOES		BASSOONS
SECOND VIOLINS	VIOLAS	DOUBLE BASSES
FIRST VIOLINS		CELLOS

Classical Orchestras mostly used Stringed Instruments

1) The most important section in a Classical orchestra is the strings. They're the dominant sound in most Classical music. The violins generally play most of the tunes.

2) The wind instruments play extra notes to fill out the harmony. When they do get the tune, they mostly double the string parts.

3) You do hear the occasional wind solo. Orchestral pieces called concertos feature one solo instrument accompanied by an orchestra.

4) In later Classical music, the woodwind section started to have a more independent role. They'd sometimes play the tune alone, and there'd be more solos. The strings were still really important though.

I find wind more uncomfortable than harmonious...

I'd love to be rich enough to have my own personal composer — it'd be like having a musical slave. Unfortunately, you're not allowed to hire one for your GCSE compositions — I think that'd be cheating.

The Classical Style

A whole page about the features of Classical music... enjoy.

Classical melodies have a Clear, Simple Structure

Classical music sounds clearer and simpler than music from other periods. This is partly because the tunes are structured in a very straightforward way, with short, balanced 2- or 4-bar phrases.

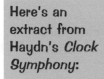

Here's an extract from Haydn's *Clock Symphony*:

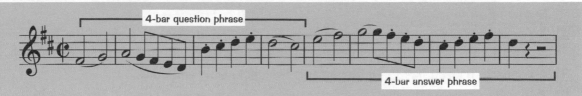

4-bar question phrase

4-bar answer phrase

And here's a bit from Mozart's *Symphony No. 40 in G minor* (your set piece), with the same balanced question and answer phrasing:

question phrase goes up in pitch

answer phrase goes down, balancing question phrase

Classical Textures are mainly Tune and Chords

1) Most Classical music has just one tune with accompanying chords. This makes the tune really stand out. It's called homophonic texture (see Section 4, Core Book).

2) These accompanying chords can be played in different ways:

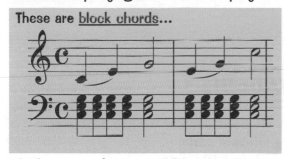

These are block chords...

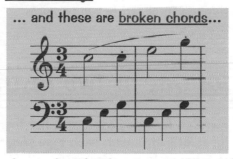

... and these are broken chords...

3) Polyphony — where several tunes weave in and out of each other — is used too, but not so often.

Classical music uses Major and Minor Keys

Classical music's always in either a major or minor key — the tonality is major or minor. Bright, cheery bits are in major keys and gloomy, sad bits are in minor keys. And...

...Classical harmony is what's known as diatonic — nearly all the notes belong to the main key.

The Beat is obvious and Easy to Follow

1) The metre in Classical music is very regular. You can happily tap your foot in time to the music.

2) The tempo stays constant — the speed of the beat stays pretty much the same all the way through, without massively speeding up or slowing down.

Classical style — a wig, tailcoat and breeches...

This is all good background to Classical music — make sure you know the key features. They're useful if you're asked to describe music from the Classical period. Make a list of them all, then learn it. Keep going back over it to check you know them off by heart. Then you can go off and have a cup of tea. Mmm tea.

Classical Structures

Concertos, sonatas and symphonies were very popular in the Classical period. You have to study one movement of a Mozart symphony, so it's important that you know some bits about symphonies.

Concertos are played by a Soloist and Orchestra

1) Concertos, symphonies and sonatas were popular Classical forms. They're covered in more detail in Section 5 in the Core Book.

2) A concerto is a piece for a soloist and orchestra. The soloist has most of the tune, and can really show off. The orchestra does get the tune too — they're not just an accompaniment.

3) A concerto usually has three movements — quick, slow and quick.

4) They often have a bit called a cadenza, where the orchestra stops and the soloist manically improvises to show everyone how brilliant they are.

5) Piano and violin concertos were most popular in the Classical period, though some composers wrote clarinet, horn and trumpet concertos too.

A Symphony is played by a Full Orchestra

1) A symphony is a massive piece. They can last more than an hour and have real impact because they use the full orchestra.

2) Symphonies usually have four movements (but some have three, and they can have more than four). The contrast between the movements is important.

3) At least one of the movements is in sonata form (see p. 19) — usually the first, and sometimes the last.

4) Haydn, Mozart and Beethoven all wrote symphonies.

Sonatas are for One or Two instruments

1) Sonatas are mostly written for one instrument, but there are some sonatas for two instruments and a few for two types of instrument, each type playing different parts.

2) A sonata usually has three or four movements, with breaks in between them.

3) A sonata has a similar structure to a symphony — it has one or more movements in sonata form.

Classical composers wrote Overtures and Suites too

1) An overture is a one-movement piece for orchestra.

2) Overtures are written as introductions to larger works like operas and ballets.

3) They use ideas, moods and musical themes from the main work to prepare the audience.

4) Classical orchestral suites are another offshoot of ballets and operas.

5) A suite is an orchestral arrangement of the music used to accompany the action on stage, put together as a separate piece of music and played at concerts.

Arches, columns, amphitheatres...

Classical composers were real masters of form and structure. They liked their music to be carefully constructed and beautifully balanced, with helpful hints to what was coming next. Ooo, I love alliteration.

Classical Structures

Sonata form is a really important structure in Classical music — most sonatas and symphonies had at least one movement in sonata form. The movement you have to study is in sonata form.

A piece in Sonata Form has Three Main Sections

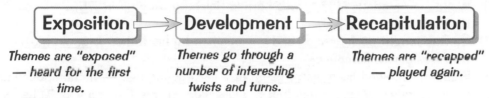

Exposition	Development	Recapitulation
Themes are "exposed" — heard for the first time.	Themes go through a number of interesting twists and turns.	Themes are "recapped" — played again.

1) The exposition has two contrasting themes. It ends in a different (but related) key to the one it started in.

2) The development keeps the piece interesting — the themes are taken through lots of variations.

3) The recapitulation pulls it all together again — the themes from the exposition are repeated. They're usually changed a bit — the composer might add ornaments (see p. 12) or shorten them a bit.

4) Composers sometimes use bridge sections between the themes and links between the main sections. They usually add a coda to finish off the piece neatly as well.

Musical Signposts tell you what's coming next

The most obvious clue that a new section is starting in Classical music is a change of key. Classical composers were also keen on dropping advance hints that a new section was about to start. These hints are called musical signposts. They're not all that easy to spot at first, but with a bit of practice you should get the hang of it:

1) Bridge passages lead smoothly into the new theme and also help prepare the new key.

2) Cadences clearly mark the end of a phrase or section, and they come at the end of a piece too. When they do, the chords used in the cadence are repeated several times, to let the audience know it's all over.

There are Standard Forms for 4-Movement Compositions

Sonatas and symphonies all follow the same basic plan. These are the traditional forms used by composers for each of the movements.

This one's left out of sonatas in three movements.

FIRST MOVEMENT	sonata form	brisk and purposeful
SECOND MOVEMENT	ternary or variation form	slower and songlike
THIRD MOVEMENT	minuet or scherzo	fairly fast and dance-like
FOURTH MOVEMENT	rondo, variation or sonata form	fast and cheerful

Simon's exposition nearly got him arrested...

Plan A: plant spies in the upper levels of transport, communication and power companies. Infiltrate the inner sanctum of said companies. Disable travel links, phone lines and internet. Cause country-wide powercut. Watch mass panic ensue. Invade Canada. From Canada, take over the world. Plan B: cinema.

Mozart — 1st Movement from Symphony No. 40 in G minor

Make sure you're <u>familiar</u> with the first movement of Mozart's *Symphony No. 40* — <u>listen</u> to it <u>over and over again</u> until you can <u>whistle</u> it in your <u>sleep</u>.

Mozart was an Austrian composer

1) <u>Wolfgang Amadeus Mozart</u> was born in <u>Salzburg</u>, <u>Austria</u> in <u>1756</u>. He died in <u>Vienna</u> in <u>1791</u>.
2) He was taught <u>performance</u> and <u>composition</u> by his father, <u>Leopold Mozart</u>, who was also a composer.
3) Wolfgang showed his <u>musical talent</u> at a very <u>young</u> age — he composed his first piece of music when he was just <u>5 years old</u>. By the time he was <u>10</u> he had <u>toured Europe</u>, performed for <u>kings</u> and <u>queens</u> and written his first <u>opera</u>.
4) He went on to write over <u>600</u> pieces of music, including <u>operas</u>, <u>masses</u>, <u>symphonies</u> and <u>concertos</u>. He also wrote smaller works, like <u>chamber music</u> and <u>string quartets</u>.
5) He's still considered to be one of the <u>greatest composers</u> that ever lived.

He wrote lots of Symphonies

1) Mozart wrote over <u>40</u> symphonies in his short life.
2) He wrote most of his symphonies before he was <u>25</u>, then took a <u>break</u> from them — he could make <u>more money</u> from composing <u>concertos</u>, and get a <u>better reputation</u> from writing <u>operas</u>.
3) He <u>returned</u> to symphonies later on — *Symphony No. 40* was written in <u>1788</u>. It's one of only two of his symphonies in a <u>minor key</u> (*Symphony No. 25* and *Symphony No. 40*, both in <u>G minor</u>).
4) He wrote *Symphony No. 40* and <u>two</u> others in just <u>6 weeks</u>.

Symphony No. 40 was written for a Small Orchestra

1) This symphony is written for a <u>fairly small orchestra</u> — there's <u>no percussion</u> at all, and the only brass instruments are the <u>French horns</u> (there are no <u>trumpets</u>).
2) The original version didn't have <u>clarinets</u> because they'd only just been invented. Mozart wrote <u>another, later version</u> that included them — it's this version that you'll be studying.

It has Four Movements

Like most symphonies, *Symphony No. 40 in G minor* has <u>four movements</u>. What's <u>unusual</u> is that Mozart uses <u>sonata form</u> (see p. 19) for <u>three</u> movements, instead of just one or two. Boy, did that bloke like sonata form.
The <u>names</u> of the movements are just the <u>tempos</u>.

FIRST MOVEMENT	*Molto Allegro* (very fast) — sonata form.	
SECOND MOVEMENT	*Andante* (walking pace) — sonata form.	
THIRD MOVEMENT	*Allegretto* (in between *andante* and *allegro*) — minuet and trio form (see p. 9).	
FOURTH MOVEMENT	*Allegro assai* (very, very fast) — sonata form.	

⟸ This is the movement you have to study for your exam.

Scream if you want to go molto allegro...

Haydn (Mozart's friend and fellow composer), described Mozart as 'the greatest composer known to me in person or by name' — that's quite a recommendation. Even if he was overly-fond of sonata form.

Mozart — 1st Movement from Symphony No. 40 in G minor

The first movement of this symphony is in sonata form. If you're a bit unsure about sonata form, have a look at p. 19 — make sure you know what the three different sections of this form are.

Bars 1-100 are the Exposition

FIRST SUBJECT (BARS 1-28)

1) The first idea lasts from bar 1 to bar 9 (there's no introduction), then the second idea is heard in bars 9-14. Bars 1-5 are shown on p. 18. Both ideas are played by the violins (the two parts are playing in octaves).
2) The first three notes of the first idea are repeated throughout the first subject — the second idea starts with these notes but a 6th higher.
3) This movement is marked *p* (*piano*) at the start, which is very unusual for a Classical symphony — they normally have a loud opening.
4) It's in G minor, but it modulates (changes key) to Bb major when the subject is repeated in bars 20-28.

TRANSITION or BRIDGE PASSAGE (BARS 28-43)

1) This section is *f* (*forte*) all the way through, with lots of *sfz* (*sforzandos*) from bar 34.
2) This section begins in Bb major, but extra chromatic notes add tension.
3) The violins play a descending sequence from bars 30-33, over a lower string tremolo with sustained notes from the upper woodwind.

SECOND SUBJECT (BARS 44-72)

1) The second subject's in Bb major, though Mozart uses a lot of chromatic notes (notes that don't fit in the key) in this bit.
2) The strings play the theme first, then the woodwind repeat it at bar 52.
3) Mozart uses ornaments (see p. 12) for the first time here — the woodwind play trills in bar 65.

CODETTA (BARS 72-100)

1) A codetta is like a mini coda — it's used to finish off the exposition section.
2) There's lots of imitation (see p. 11) between the clarinet and the bassoon.
3) The key changes back from Bb major to G minor at the end of this bit.
4) The whole of the exposition is repeated.

The Development section is bars 101-164

1) All the music in the development section is based on the first idea from the exposition.
2) The harmonies are more chromatic in this bit.
3) The development section begins in F# minor, but it explores lots of different keys — e.g. bars 118-128.
4) From bar 140, Mozart uses lots of pedal points (see p. 15).

Bars 164-299 are the Recapitulation

1) The first subject (bars 164-184) is exactly the same as in the exposition.
2) The bridge passage is much longer this time — it lasts from bar 184 to bar 227. It passes through quite a few keys — including Eb major, F minor and D major. It's polyphonic — in bars 202-210, there's a sequence being played in canon between Violin I and the lower strings.
3) The second subject (bars 227-260) is shared between the woodwind and the strings. This time it's in G minor, and there are some ascending chromatic notes in the bass parts from bar 245.
4) The coda (bars 260-299) is an extended version of the codetta. It finishes with four G minor chords — it's really obvious that the movement's finished.

A codetta is a baby coda...

Listen to the movement again, and try and follow it on the score. Make sure you know where each section starts and finishes, and pay attention to the different features of each bit. Then listen to it again and again.

The Romantic Period

The Romantic period... <u>hearts</u>, <u>flowers</u>, <u>moonlit walks</u> on the beach. Actually <u>no</u>. The Romantic period isn't about kissing and cuddling, it's about how <u>passionate emotions</u> can be <u>expressed</u> through <u>art</u> and <u>music</u>.

The Romantic Period was in the 19th Century

1) The <u>Romantic period</u> was from about <u>1820-1900</u> (but there's a bit of an <u>overlap</u> between different musical periods).
2) <u>Writers</u>, <u>artists</u> and <u>composers</u> at this time were portraying <u>feelings</u> and <u>nature</u> in their work. They wanted to show <u>contrasts</u> — like <u>love</u> and <u>hate</u>, <u>happiness</u> and <u>grief</u>, and <u>life</u> and <u>death</u>.
3) As well as being inspired by the <u>natural world</u>, they were fascinated by <u>supernatural</u> ideas.
4) Composers wrote music based on <u>poems</u> and <u>paintings</u>, and also used their music to <u>tell stories</u>.
5) <u>Tchaikovsky</u>, <u>Brahms</u> and <u>Chopin</u> were all Romantic composers. Some of <u>Beethoven</u>'s later pieces also fitted into the Romantic period.

Romantic music is more Dramatic than Classical

1) Romantic composers used a <u>wide range</u> of <u>dynamics</u>, with lots of <u>sudden changes</u> — in one bar, the music could change from *ppp* to *fff* and back again. They also used a lot of <u>sforzandos</u> and <u>accents</u> as well — it made the music very <u>dramatic</u>.
2) To make the music more <u>expressive</u>, composers gave <u>extra instructions</u> — as well as <u>tempo markings</u>, they would include instructions like *dolce* (sweetly), *amoroso* (lovingly) or *agitato* (agitated).
3) There were more <u>tempo changes</u> — a piece might <u>change speeds</u> lots of times within the <u>same section</u>. Musicians in this period used *rubato* as well — it means '<u>robbed time</u>' and it's when performers <u>speed up</u> a little in one phrase and <u>slow down</u> in another to make up for it. It gives them the <u>freedom</u> to be more <u>expressive</u>.
4) Composers added <u>extra notes</u> to <u>chords</u> to make the <u>harmonies</u> more <u>interesting</u> — they used <u>7ths</u>, <u>9ths</u>, <u>11ths</u> and <u>13ths</u> (9ths, 11ths and 13ths are just <u>2nds</u>, <u>4ths</u> and <u>6ths</u> but an <u>octave higher</u>). They helped create <u>dissonance</u> (clashing notes), which helped them show emotions like <u>pain</u> and <u>misery</u>.
5) There was a lot of <u>virtuoso playing</u> — composers wrote <u>technically difficult music</u> to give performers the chance to <u>show off</u>. It was very <u>exciting</u> to watch and listen to. <u>Rachmaninoff</u> and <u>Liszt</u> wrote <u>solo piano music</u> that had to be written on <u>four staves</u> as there were so many notes to play.
6) Lots of Romantic composers were very <u>proud</u> of the countries they came from — they used <u>folk tunes</u> and <u>dance rhythms</u> from their <u>homelands</u> to show their <u>national pride</u>. Tchaikovsky used the <u>French</u> and <u>Russian national anthems</u> in his *1812 Overture*.

The orchestra Developed in the Romantic Period

1) <u>Orchestras</u> got much <u>bigger</u> — extra instruments were added to all sections of the orchestra, especially <u>woodwind</u> and <u>percussion</u>.
2) <u>Brass</u> instruments were able to play <u>more notes</u> as they now had <u>valves</u>.
3) All these changes meant that composers could write music with a larger range of <u>texture</u>, <u>timbre</u> and <u>dynamics</u>.
4) The <u>development</u> of the <u>piano</u> (see p. 23) meant that it became a much more <u>popular</u> and <u>important</u> instrument. Lots of piano music was written in the Romantic period.

If music be the food of love — play on...

Make sure you know some <u>key features</u> of Romantic music — you'll need to be able to <u>spot</u> them in the <u>set piece</u>. Listen out for <u>dynamic contrasts</u> and <u>interesting harmonies</u> in Chopin's *Raindrop* prelude.

The Romantic Period

The piano was definitely one of the most important instruments in the Romantic period.

The Piano Developed in the Romantic Period

The piano's been around since the 18th century, but the developments in the 19th century made it really popular with Romantic composers.

SIZE: the piano changed shape a bit and got bigger (and louder). This meant it had a bigger dynamic range.

STRINGS: the strings inside were both thicker and longer, making a fuller tone. They were also pulled tighter, so they were more tense.

KEYS: the number of keys (and notes) increased to just over 7 octaves. Composers now had a larger range in pitch to compose for.

FRAME: the frame used to be made of wood, but was now made of metal (to cope with the new strings). This made it easier to transport them.

PEDALS: both pedals (the sustain pedal that holds notes on and the soft pedal) became more effective. Some modern pianos have three pedals — the third pedal allows some notes to be held on while others are not.

HAMMERS: the hammers were given a felt covering (instead of a leather one). This made the tone softer and more rounded.

Melodies were the Focus of piano pieces

1) In Romantic piano pieces, the melody was the most important part. Melodies were often marked cantabile — to be played in a singing style.
2) There were lots of virtuosic sections and cadenzas (see p. 18) to give the pianist chance to show off.
3) The music had a large range of dynamics, articulation and tone. Pianists had to use the pedals a lot to get the right sounds.
4) The accompaniment was often broken chords (see p. 17), but unlike many Classical pieces, the broken chords would be spread across several octaves.

Preludes were popular piano pieces

Preludes were originally the bit of music that came before the main piece. During the Romantic period, they had become popular as stand-alone pieces.

1) Debussy wrote preludes for piano. There's one in his Suite Bergamasque.
2) Liszt and Rachmaninoff wrote some very tricky piano preludes.
3) Chopin wrote a set of 24 piano preludes, one in each of the 24 keys. They're all pretty short — the longest is only 90 bars long, and the shortest lasts for just 13 bars. They don't follow set structures, though there are motifs (short musical ideas) that crop up in more than one prelude. Your set work is Prelude No. 15 in D flat major — also called the Raindrop prelude.

I'll have soup as a prelude to my dinner...

Pianos were popular because they were so versatile — with a range of over seven octaves, composers had fewer limitations when they were composing. The newly-developed piano could play a wide range of dynamics, and the pedals could be used to change the tone of the instrument too. Perfect for the Romantics.

Chopin — Prelude No. 15 in D flat Major

Your set piece is Chopin's *Prelude No. 15 in D flat Major*. It's also known as the *Raindrop* prelude.

Chopin was a Polish Composer

1) Frédéric Chopin was born in Poland in 1810 — lots of his music uses Polish folk tunes and dance rhythms. He died in Paris in 1849.
2) He made a name for himself in Vienna before moving to Paris.
3) As well as composing, he also performed and taught music.
4) He composed a lot of piano music, and had a reputation as a 'tragic' Romantic composer, because he was ill a lot, and died young.

The Raindrop Prelude is in Ternary Form

1) *Prelude No. 15 in D♭ Major* is quite short (it's only 89 bars long) but can be divided up into four main sections. The first, Section A lasts from bars 1-27, and Section B from bars 28-75. A short bit of Section A is repeated in bars 76-81, then the piece finishes with a coda in bars 81-89. Unlike some of the other preludes, it has a clear structure — it's in ternary form (see p. 9).
2) Section A is in D♭ major, while Section B is in C♯ minor. Enharmonically, C♯ minor is the tonic minor of D♭ major (as D♭ is the enharmonic equivalent of C♯). Chopin explores other keys in both sections — this is typical of Romantic music.
3) It's called the *Raindrop* prelude because of a repeated quaver A♭ in the left-hand part (it changes to a G♯ when the key changes to C♯ minor). This note is repeated throughout the piece.

Section A introduces the 'Raindrop'

1) This prelude is marked *sostenuto* — it doesn't just mean sustained here, but it should also have a slow, held back tempo. The pianist has to use the pedal a lot — it helps sustain the notes.
2) You can hear the 'raindrop' note in the first bar, and it continues throughout the piece.
3) The first melodic phrase lasts 4 bars and is marked *p* (*piano* — quiet). The first three notes of the melody are descending — like raindrops. In the bar 3, the melody is harmonised in 6ths. These four bars are repeated with no changes (except for the last beat of the phrase, which leads into the new phrase). There's an ornament (see p. 12) in the fourth bar — it's a turn written out in full. The turn isn't played in the 8th bar.

These are the 'raindrop' notes.

This means 'press the pedal'.

This means 'release it'.

4) Another melodic idea starts in the last two quavers of bar 8. It's a four-bar melody and the key moves towards A♭ minor. It's followed by a variation of the tune.
5) From bars 14-20, the 'raindrop' note is played on an F, not an A♭.
6) The melody goes through B♭ minor (the relative minor of D♭ major), then back to D♭ major for the last few bars of this section, where you can hear the opening melody again.

Raindrops keep falling on my piano...

Try and follow the phrases marked on the score as you listen to the piece. It'll help you spot where the sections start and finish. Listen out for the modulations (key changes) as well. Section B's on the next page.

Chopin — Prelude No. 15 in D flat Major

This page carries on with the <u>analysis</u> of the *Raindrop* prelude — it picks up at <u>Section B</u>, which starts at bar 28 and finishes at bar 75.

Section B is in C♯ Minor

1) Section B is very <u>different</u> to Section A. It's in a <u>minor key</u>, and sounds much more <u>dramatic</u>.
2) The <u>melody</u>'s in <u>crotchets</u> in the <u>bass part</u>. The melody is played <u>underneath</u> the 'raindrop' notes — in this section, they're <u>G♯s</u>. It's marked *sotto voce*, which means '<u>in an undertone</u>' — it should be <u>soft</u> and <u>quiet</u>.

3) In bar 35, Chopin starts to build up the <u>texture</u> by <u>doubling</u> the 'raindrop' in <u>octaves</u> — it feels <u>powerful</u>.
4) The <u>dynamics</u> start to <u>build up gradually</u> until bar 43, where the music drops back down to <u>p</u>. It then gets louder again, building up to *ff* (*fortissimo*) in bar 56. There are lots of <u>accents</u> in Section B (see bars 40-43 and 56-59). This is quite a <u>contrast</u> to Section A, which was *p* all the way through with no accents.
5) In bars 60-63, the melody is quite <u>similar</u> to the start of Section B, but some of the <u>note lengths</u> have been <u>augmented</u> (made longer). This makes it feel <u>slow</u> and <u>heavy</u>.
6) In bars 64-67, the <u>repeated G♯s</u> in the top line form an <u>inverted pedal</u> (a <u>pedal point</u> is one that is <u>held on</u> or repeated, usually in the <u>bass part</u>. An inverted pedal is a <u>held note</u> in the <u>top part</u>).
7) Although this section's in <u>C♯ minor</u>, Chopin <u>explores</u> other keys — the <u>harmonies</u> pass through <u>G♯ minor</u> and <u>F♯ minor</u>.
8) Bar 75 (the last bar of Section B) is a <u>transition bar</u> between Section B and the repeat of Section A. The last 4 quavers of bar 75 prepare for the <u>key change</u> in the next bar.

Part of Section A is Repeated

1) In bar 76, the piece <u>returns</u> to the key of <u>D♭ major</u> and repeats Section A.
2) The <u>opening phrase</u> is played again, just with a slightly different <u>ornament</u> — it's more <u>chromatic</u>, and has 10 notes instead of 7.
3) Chopin suggests that the piece is coming to the end by using the term *smorzando* (which means '<u>dying away</u>') in bar 79.
4) In bar 81, the melody is <u>cut short</u> to make way for the <u>coda</u>.

The Coda finishes the piece

1) The <u>coda</u> starts on the last beat of bar 81, and lasts until bar 89 (the end of the piece). The <u>melodic line</u> in bars 81-83 has the <u>highest notes</u> of the prelude. These are also the <u>only</u> bars that are <u>not</u> accompanied by the 'raindrop' quavers.
2) In bar 84, the 'raindrops' <u>come back</u> on the dominant note (A♭) until the final tonic (D♭) chord.
3) The coda starts off *f* then drops down to *p*. The final two bars are *pp* (*pianissimo*), the <u>quietest</u> part of the whole piece.
4) The piece <u>slows down</u> towards the end with a gentle *ritenuto*.

I'm going to augment my tea-break...

Listen out for the <u>contrasts</u> between Section A and Section B. Make sure you can spot the <u>key changes</u> and the <u>changes in dynamics</u>. Section B sounds a lot more <u>dramatic</u> than Section A, which is quite <u>calm</u>.

Revision Summary

Phew, this section's almost over now. Remember that the most important part of the Listening Exam is showing how well you know those good old set pieces. So make yourself a nice cup of herbal tea, put on your pink fluffy carpet slippers and settle down on the sofa with this relaxing revision summary. It might look like a plain old revision summary to the untrained eye but it's actually more exciting than watching paint dry and it could well help you get a better mark in your exam. Can't say fairer than that.

1) Give the approximate dates of the Baroque and Classical periods.
2) How do the dynamics change in Baroque music?
3) What is a basso continuo and what instruments would normally play it?
4) Which baroque structure can be described as AABBAA?
5) In theme and variation form, what is the theme?
6) What is the main difference between theme and variation form and ground bass form?
7) Explain what each of these terms means:
   a) melodic inversion   b) retrograde   c) ostinato.
8) Name three different ornaments used by Baroque composers and explain what they are.
9) What is an appoggiatura?
10) Describe the main difference between sacred and secular music.
11) What are the three main types of songs in Baroque choral music?
12) Write down three features of an oratorio.
13) In what year did Handel write 'Messiah'?
14) What are the three sections of 'Messiah' about?
15) Describe where the *And the Glory of the Lord* chorus comes in 'Messiah'.
16) Write down the words that make up the *And the Glory of the Lord* chorus.
17) Describe the way the key modulates in *And the Glory of the Lord*.
18) Write down two features of the last four bars of *And the Glory of the Lord* which make the piece sound finished.
19) Name two famous Classical composers.
20) What is the most important section in a Classical orchestra?
21) Classical music usually has a homophonic texture. What does this mean?
22) Write down two of the differences between symphonies and concertos.
23) What are the three main sections in sonata form?
24) What instruments did Mozart write *Symphony No. 40* for?
25) What key is *Symphony No. 40* written in?
26) What is the first movement of *Symphony No. 40* called and what form is it in?
27) How does Mozart develop the Exposition in bars 101-164 of *Symphony No. 40*?
28) Write down four ideas which inspired Romantic composers.
29) How did piano playing change in the Romantic period?
30) What is a Prelude?
31) Why is Chopin's *Prelude No. 15 in D flat Major* described as the *Raindrop* prelude?
32) Briefly describe the structure of the *Raindrop* prelude.
33) What key is Section A of the *Raindrop* prelude in? What key is Section B in?
34) How do the dynamics change from Section A to Section B in the *Raindrop* prelude?

Expressionism

In the 1900s composers started monkeying around with the way music was written.
They dumped Classical-style tonal music — they hardly ever used major and minor scales.

Romantic Composers started the move Away from Tonality

The big changes to art music (that's music that was written down, rather than folk music) in the twentieth century didn't just appear suddenly. They developed from changes that were already happening during the Romantic period.

> The Romantic period runs roughly from 1820 to 1900 — it fills the gap between Classical music and the twentieth century. There's more about the Romantic period on p. 22-23.

1) Classical music is tonal — the key a piece is written in gives it a definite character.

2) Romantic composers used a lot of chromatic notes and chords — notes and chords that didn't belong to the main key of a melody.

More chromatics... I must have more chromatics...

3) The Romantics bunged in so many chromatics that their music started to lose the character of the main key.

4) By the early twentieth century a lot of music sounded like it didn't belong to any key at all. Music that doesn't sound like it comes from any particular key is called atonal.

The change from tonal to atonal music doesn't sound that dramatic on paper, but it was a really big change. The old forms like binary, ternary and rondo (see Section 2 for more on these) relied on fixed keys to create contrast between the different sections. Now fixed keys were gone, so were all the old ways of structuring music.

Arnold Schoenberg's music was Expressionist

1) Arnold Schoenberg was born in Vienna, in Austria, in 1874. He was a composer, conductor and teacher at the University of Vienna. His early music had a late-Romantic feel. He followed composers like Wagner by adding lots of chromatics to his piece.

2) In the early twentieth century he became interested in the ideas of expressionist painters like Wassily Kandinsky. Expressionists believed that art should express your inner feelings without being restricted by conventional forms. The practical result of this in Kandinsky's paintings was abstract shapes and moody colours.

3) In Schoenberg's music the practical result was his move towards atonal music (his earlier music was tonal). He felt traditional tonal music was too restrictive. It couldn't express the full range of human emotions — especially not the more unhappy ones. His music had lots of dissonance (clashing notes) that didn't resolve (move to a non-clashing note) straight away.

4) One of Schoenberg's first atonal pieces, *Three Piano Pieces*, was first performed in 1909.

> **EXPRESSIONIST MUSIC:**
> - is intensely emotional
> - has angular, spiky melodies
> - has lots of dissonance (chords with clashing notes)
> - is mainly atonal (doesn't sound like it's in a particular key)
> - has contrasting dynamics
> - doesn't really have cadences, repetition or sequences
> - is always changing — it never sticks with any one musical idea for long

5) Schoenberg invented serialism (see p. 30) in 1923.

Chromatics, chromatics — nothing but chromatics...

Make sure you know the difference between tonal and atonal music, and can identify it when you hear it. Music that's written in two keys at the same time is called bitonal — it's a bit different to atonal music.

Arnold Schoenberg — Peripetie

Schoenberg's music sounds a bit weird. You need to know the features that make it weird.

Schoenberg's music changed from Tonal to Atonal

1) Schoenberg wrote a string sextet called 'Verklärte Nacht' in 1899. It's tonal, but has lots of chromaticism in it.

2) His first orchestral work was 'Pelleas und Melisande' in 1903.

3) He wrote a suite called 'Five Orchestral Pieces' ('Fünf Orchesterstücke') in 1909. One movement's called *Peripetie* — you need to know about this one for your exam (it's covered in more detail on the next page). By this point, most of Schoenberg's work was atonal (including this suite).

4) In 'Pierrot-Lunaire' (1912), an atonal piece for soprano and chamber orchestra, Schoenberg used a half-singing, half-speaking vocal technique (Sprechstimme) to deliver gruesome lines. Movements have cheery titles like *Homesickness*, *Song of the Gallows* and *Decapitation*. At one point, Pierrot drills into another character's brain. Nice.

5) '5 Pieces for Piano' (1923) was one of his first serial works (see p. 30).

Peripetie is an Expressionist piece

1) *Peripetie* is the fourth movement of Schoenberg's 'Five Orchestral Pieces'. It was originally written in 1909, but he revised it in 1922 and 1949. It's an example of one of Schoenberg's Expressionist pieces.

2) He didn't want to give each movement a title, but gave in because his publisher thought it was a good idea. He deliberately chose names that didn't give away too much about the piece — he thought the music should speak for itself. The other movements are called *Premonitions*, *The Past*, *Summer Morning by a Lake: Chord Colours* and *Obbligato Recitative*.

3) *Peripetie* comes from a Greek word that means 'sudden changes'. It's very different to the one before it, and there are lots of changes of timbre and texture within the piece (see p. 29).

Peripetie was written for a Big Orchestra

1) By the end of the Romantic period, orchestras were huge. They'd often have full woodwind sections and lots of percussion.

2) Schoenberg wrote his '5 Orchestral Pieces' for a big orchestra. It allowed him to make lots of contrasts in texture, timbre and dynamics.

3) *Peripetie* needs a massive woodwind section — it's written for quadruple woodwind. Quadruple woodwind is three flutes and a piccolo, three oboes and a cor anglais, three clarinets and a bass clarinet and three bassoons and a contrabassoon.

4) It also needs a big brass section — six horns, three trumpets, four trombones and a tuba. There's lots of percussion as well, including timpani, cymbals and a xylophone. The string section was fairly standard though.

5) When Schoenberg revised the piece in 1949, he changed the instrumentation a bit. He used fewer instruments, reducing the number of clarinets, oboes, bassoons, horns and trombones. This made it a bit more accessible for smaller orchestras.

6) The parts are tricky — lots of instruments play very high or very low. There are big leaps in pitch too, sometimes more than an octave.

I feel a premonition — that girl's gonna make me fall...

Schoenberg was a bit of a revolutionary. He was also a bit of an oddbod — apparently he had a fear of the number 13. He actually died on a Friday 13th, so maybe he had reason to be scared. I'm scared of buttons.

Arnold Schoenberg — Peripetie

'Peripetie' is only a short piece (it lasts about 2 minutes), but Schoenberg manages to cram a lot into it.

It has an Unusual Structure

1) Schoenberg didn't use a conventional structure — there isn't an obvious melody.
   He uses melodic fragments and complicated, fragmented rhythms. Each fragment is based on a
   hexachord — a group of six notes from the 12 different semitones. The six semitones not used in the
   hexachord are called the complement.

2) It's atonal (not written in a key). Schoenberg uses the hexachords to create dissonances (clashing notes).

3) Peripetie's almost in rondo form (see p. 9) — the same melodic idea returns a few times. Some people say
   it's a free rondo. The sections are different lengths, and the textures and tempos change in each section.

4) This movement's marked Sehr rasch (very fast) and it's only 66 bars long. Schoenberg gives other
   instructions during the piece, like heftig (passionate) and ruhiger (calmer).

5) It's an example of Klangfarbenmelodie (a German word that means 'tone-colour-melody').
   The name was made up by Schoenberg, and it's a technique he used to break up a melody
   by passing it round different parts. It gives the tune variations in the timbre (tone colour).

The Instrumentation changes in each Section

The free rondo structure is made up of five sections — it goes ABA'CA'' (A' and A'' are variations on Section A).

SECTION A (BARS 1-18)   Every instrument in the orchestra gets to play in Section A, but only for a
bar or two at a time. The instruments play in groups — the clarinets, bass clarinet and bassoons play
one melodic fragment, followed by the trumpets and trombones, and so on — the little bits of tune are
passed around the orchestra. This section starts off very loud, but drops down to pp in bar 6.

SECTION B (BARS 18-34)   Again, all the instrument in the orchestra get to play in this section, but this
time most parts play alone. They're all playing different rhythms, and the parts overlap. Towards the
end of this section, almost every instrument's playing at the same time, though not the same rhythms
— it has a very thick texture. Section B starts off very quietly, but the dynamics build up quickly.

SECTION A' (BARS 35-43)   The hexachord from bar 8 is played again by the horns.

SECTION C (BARS 44-58)   This section has a thin texture — there are solo lines for the cello and
double bass. There a few loud semiquaver triplets, but most of this section is calm and quiet.

SECTION A'' (BARS 59-66)   Peripetie finishes with another variation of Section A. The instrumentation
builds up from just the clarinets and strings until the whole orchestra plays a fff chord in bar 64.
The piece finishes with a pp chord in the horns and double bass.

There are lots of Contrasts

1) Peripetie is a very dramatic piece. Schoenberg uses lots of sudden changes in texture, dynamics and
   timbre to make it sound exciting.

2) There's a wide range of extreme dynamics — from pp to fff. The dynamics change very quickly.

3) There are sudden changes of texture. In some places, lots of instruments play different parts, all weaving
   in and out of each other (polyphony or counterpoint). At other points, the texture is much thinner and
   you can hear a solo instrument, like a clarinet or flute.

4) Schoenberg changes the timbre a lot as well. There are quick changes between families of instruments,
   like woodwind, strings and brass. This changes the sound of the piece.

5) He uses lots of different note lengths — from demi-semiquavers to semibreves.

Schoenberg — what a drama queen...

This music was supposed to express the composer's feelings — it makes you wonder what was going
through his head when he wrote weird-sounding stuff like this. He must have had lots of nightmares.

Serialism

Schoenberg <u>invented</u> a new way of composing called <u>serialism</u>. Your set piece isn't a serialist piece, but it's useful to know about it in case you want to use it in one of your <u>compositions</u>.

Schoenberg Replaced tonality with Serialism

1) Once Schoenberg had done away with the conventions of using major and minor keys he needed to find a new way to <u>structure</u> his music. The method he came up with was called <u>serialism</u>.

2) Serialism meant putting some element of the piece into a series or order — it could be a set order of <u>volume changes</u> or a particular set of <u>notes</u> — his first works concentrated on ordering the notes.

3) To compose a piece, Schoenberg would start by arranging the <u>12 chromatic notes</u> of an octave into a <u>set order</u>. It was known as the <u>12-Tone System</u>. The initial arrangement is called the <u>Prime Order</u>:

The Prime Order is Rearranged

The <u>next step</u> is <u>rearranging the Prime Order</u>. There are several fixed ways of doing this...

PRIME ORDER IN RETROGRADE
Notes in reverse order

PRIME ORDER INVERTED
Intervals between notes
turned upside down

PRIME ORDER IN RETROGRADE INVERSION
Inverted notes in reverse order

The four different versions of the Prime Order can be <u>transposed</u> — each one can start on any of the 12 different notes. This creates <u>48</u> different sets of notes to work with. These sequences of notes are called <u>rows</u> — they're written out <u>horizontally</u>, not vertically (like chords).

The Snippets of melody Combine as a complete piece

Once Schoenberg had all his variations on the Prime Order, he could use these patterns of notes as <u>building blocks</u> to create a complete piece of music.

1) Notes from the prime order, or variations, can be played in the <u>bass line</u> or <u>melody</u> and in <u>any octave</u>.

2) Groups of notes can be piled up to make <u>chords</u>. Notes that were next door to each other in the original rows would be played all at once by different instruments. This is called <u>verticalisation</u> — notes that were written out horizontally in the rows would be written out <u>vertically</u> in the score.

3) The prime order could be designed to create familiar chords like <u>triads</u>, or <u>cluster chords</u> with notes really close together.

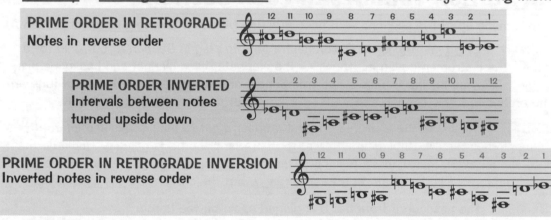

cluster chord

FAC triad

...serialism fell apart in retrograde inversion

Serialist music sounds like lots of little <u>random snippets</u> — you don't get long sweeps of melody or a steady rhythm. It's pretty <u>complicated</u> to write, so most pieces are only for <u>small groups</u> of instruments.

Minimalism

Minimalist painting is painting with just a few lines or squares. Minimalist <u>music</u> is music that just changes a <u>tiny subtle bit</u> at a time. Some people might call it boring — don't put that in the exam.

Minimalism builds music out of Loops

1) Minimalism is a <u>Western art music</u> style that developed during the <u>1960s</u> and <u>1970s</u>.
2) It's a lot <u>simpler</u> than expressionist music — it's easier to hear what's going on.
3) It's made up of constantly repeated patterns called <u>loops</u>. The loops are <u>short</u> and <u>simple</u>, but the final music can get quite <u>complicated</u> — especially the <u>rhythm</u>.
4) There's <u>no real tune</u> — you can't sing along to minimalist music.
5) The <u>harmonies</u> are made by <u>layering patterns</u> one on top of the other. They take a <u>long time</u> to <u>change</u>.
6) Some of the 'big names' in minimalism are <u>Steve Reich</u> (see p. 33), <u>Philip Glass</u> and <u>Terry Riley</u>.

These are the main Techniques for Changing the Loops

These different ways of changing the loop patterns are used in most minimalist pieces:

NOTES ARE GRADUALLY ADDED OR TAKEN AWAY

One note is <u>added</u> on each repetition of the pattern — this is called <u>additive melody</u>.

Another similar idea is to <u>replace one note with a rest</u>, or one rest with a note on each repetition.

THE NOTES OF THE PATTERN CHANGE OVER TIME

This technique's called <u>metamorphosis</u> — an unnecessarily long word for 'changing shape'. Tiny changes to <u>one note</u>, or <u>one bit of the rhythm</u>, are made in each repetition.

Often the changes go <u>full circle</u>, so the pattern ends up the <u>same</u> or nearly the same as it was at the start.

ADDING OR REMOVING NOTES OR RESTS

Two or more performers start with the <u>same pattern</u>, but one has an extra rest or note, making it a different length. They move gradually <u>out of sync</u> and then gradually back in. The proper name for this is <u>phase shifting</u>.

Classic 90s dance act Orbital used phase shifting on the album Orbital 2. In the song Time Becomes, two versions of the phrase "where time becomes a loop" are played simultaneously. They start off in sync, but one's got a bigger gap at the end, so they go gradually out of phase, then gradually back in phase. It's a pretty cool album, if a tad ancient.

LAYERING DIFFERENT-LENGTH PATTERNS TOGETHER

This one's called 'layering'. You play loops of <u>different lengths</u>, e.g. a 4-beat loop and a 5-beat loop, <u>at the same time</u>. You get a similar effect to phase-shifting — the patterns move <u>apart</u> then come back <u>together</u>.

Minimalism

Have you seen a film called _The Piano_? This woman gets her finger chopped off by an axe, has an affair with a man in all-over body tattoos and nearly drowns. And it has a minimalist soundtrack.

Music Technology plays a big part in minimalism

Minimalism has always used a lot of electronic bits and bobs to put music together. When composers first started writing minimalist music in the 1960s, they had a bit of a challenge on their hands, because music technology was a lot less sophisticated than it is today...

1) The repeated loops were played using old-fashioned tape recorders — the ones you see in old spy films with two massive wheels for the tape.

2) Composers made loops by carefully cutting a tape so it just had the bits of music they wanted, then sticking the cut ends together. The loop was played by running it out of the tape player and around something smooth, like a bottle or mike stand, so it could keep going round and round.

> Steve Reich and Terry Riley are two of the minimalist composers who used this technique for looping.

3) They didn't just use loops of music. They made loop recordings of words and other noises too — it's a bit like modern sampling.

4) The different loops were put together using multitrack recording. They were recorded, one on top of another, to create the layered sound of minimalism.

5) Even live performances of minimalist music often make use of recorded backing tracks, played alongside the live instruments.

> When you first listen to minimalist music it sounds like it hardly changes at all, but as you get used to it you'll start to spot the tiny changes to the repeated loops.

Minimalism uses musical ideas from All Over the World

Minimalists didn't just sit around in libraries waiting for inspiration to strike. Most of them have borrowed ideas from other countries and other cultures.

> West African music is based mainly on the rhythm. The master drummer leads changes in the patterns.

> West African music uses complex cross-rhythms.

> Gamelan (from Indonesia) has layered parts, all playing versions of the same tune, but at different times.

POLYRHYTHM

RHYTHM MORE IMPORTANT THAN TUNE

LAYERING

MINIMALIST MUSIC

HARMONIES CHANGE SLOWLY

> There's more on African drumming and Indian raga in Section 5.

LOOPING

PIECES LONG AND HYPNOTIC

> Gamelan doesn't use harmony at all.

> Most non-Western music's based on looping, e.g. the tala rhythm in raga is a constant loop.

> Some Indian and gamelan pieces go on for days.

> The drone in raga plays the same harmony all the way through.

Tune, tone, lone, line, lint, lent, bent, belt, bell, bull, dull...

Minimalism can take a bit of getting used to, because the tune just isn't that important. It's those tiny continual changes to the rhythm and texture that you're supposed to listen out for. On the plus side though — once you know what the changes are, you're sorted for the exam.

Section Three — AoS2: Music in the 20th Century

Steve Reich — 3rd Movement from Electric Counterpoint

Steve Reich is an American composer. He's won lots of awards — including a Grammy.

Steve Reich has composed a lot of Minimalist music

1) Reich was born in New York in 1936. He had piano lessons when he was young, then started learning the drums when he was 14.
2) He did a degree in Philosophy, then studied composition with the modernist composer Luciano Berio.
3) His music is influenced by jazz and non-Western ideas, like African drumming (see p. 62-64) and Balinese Gamelan.
4) He had a go at writing serial music (see p.30), but preferred writing tonal music (music that's written in a key). After meeting the minimalist composer Terry Riley in the 1960s, Reich began writing minimalist compositions.

He's written music for Instruments, Voices and Tape

1) One of his best-known works is a piece called *Different Trains*. It was written in 1988 and is a reaction to the Holocaust. It uses samples of people talking about train journeys, then imitates their voices with instruments.
2) He wrote a piece of music for people clapping (called *Clapping Music*) in 1972. It's for 2 people — one claps a steady rhythm throughout the piece. The other claps the same pattern, but shifts it by one quaver every few bars. It's an example of phase shifting (see p. 31).
3) *Vermont Counterpoint* (1982) is for flute and pre-recorded tape.
4) *New York Counterpoint* (1985) is for clarinet and pre-recorded tape. The recorded parts can also be performed by live clarinetists.

Electric Counterpoint is performed by One Guitarist

1) *Electric Counterpoint* was written for the jazz guitarist Pat Metheny in 1987. It has three movements — you need to know about the third movement.
2) The third movement has 7 electric guitars and 2 electric bass guitars, as well as the solo guitar part. The whole piece should be performed by a single guitarist — they play along with a multitrack recording of the other parts (called 'ensemble parts') made before the performance.
3) The movements don't have titles — they're just marked ♩ = 192, ♩ = 96 and ♩ = 192. People tend to call them 'Fast', 'Slow' and 'Fast'. The middle movement's half the speed of the others, so there's a constant pulse. The guitarist shouldn't pause between movements, but go straight from one to the next.
4) The third movement is 140 bars long and lasts about 4 and a half minutes. It's in 3/2 (3 minim beats per bar), but at some points, a few guitars (including the live part) play in 12/8 while the others stay in 3/2. The parts still fit together because both time signatures can be divided into 12 quavers per bar.
5) It's made up of short patterns (or riffs) that are repeated lots of times. A repeated pattern like this is called an ostinato.
6) The timbre (tone colour) of the piece doesn't change much because it only uses guitars and bass guitars, which all have a similar sound. The parts all blend together.

Minimalism — what's the (counter)point...

Gosh, imagine recording nine different parts, then playing another part live over the top of them. It'd be awful if you realised you'd made a mistake on the first part you'd recorded, wouldn't it.

Steve Reich — 3rd Movement from Electric Counterpoint

Just one more page on *Electric Counterpoint* then you're done with minimalism forever. Well, until the exam.

Reich uses Looping to build up Layers

1) Each different part is pre-recorded onto a tape loop (or computer loop these days). These parts are overdubbed (recorded on top of one another) using multitracking in a studio to build up the layers. The performer then plays the live part over the top of the recording.

2) The music's repetitive — the same loops are repeated in the ensemble parts (this makes the music sound more hypnotic). At some points (like bars 20-35), the solo guitar's melody is made up of notes that the ensemble parts are playing. It takes its first two notes from guitar 1, its third note from guitar 2, etc.

3) Four of the ensemble parts play the same riff throughout the piece. One guitar starts off playing it alone, then the others come in one by one. They all play it at different times — they're in canon (like a round).

4) When it first comes in, guitar 3's part is built up by a technique called note addition (or additive melody — see p. 31). It starts off playing just a few notes of the riff, then two or three notes are added each time it's played until the whole riff is heard. It starts in bar 10, but doesn't play the whole riff until bar 15.

Electric Counterpoint is Polyphonic

1) As well as the canonic one-bar riff (see point 3 above), Reich builds up another canon between the solo part and the other three ensemble guitars (this first starts in bar 36). They play a repeated strummed chord sequence.

2) The texture is polyphonic — it's made up of two or more independent parts being played at the same time. The parts fit together harmonically. The two canons going on at the same time make the polyphony more complex and interesting.

3) The counterpoint is really obvious in the sections where some parts are playing in 3/2 and the others in 12/8 (like bars 82-85). One canon is being played with three (minim) beats in a bar, and the other with four (dotted crochet) beats in a bar.

The piece Changes between Two Keys

1) This movement of *Electric Counterpoint* changes between E minor and C minor. The first modulation (key change) happens about halfway through the piece (in bar 74), but there are another 13 before the end. These key changes happen more frequently as the piece builds up — some only last for two or three bars. The harmony is quite static (the chords don't change very often).

2) Changes in the time signature (from 3/2 to 12/8 and back) in the solo and bass guitar parts happen more often towards the end of the piece as well. It feels like they're switching between three and four beats in a bar. The main part of the piece is in 3/2 though.

3) There are lots of changes in dynamics, mainly in the solo part, which fades in and out during the piece. The four ensemble parts playing the first riff stay at a constant *mf* throughout, but the other parts have some diminuendos. It finishes with a *fortissimo* (*ff*) climax from the solo part.

Minimalism — enough to drive you loopy...

This page is a bit tricky, but it's really important. It's definitely worth going over again to check you understand how the piece is put together. Have another listen to the piece to see how the techniques are applied.

Songs from Musicals

Musicals are a lighter, more modern version of opera. They've been developing since the 19th century.

Musicals have Songs, Dialogue and Dances

1) Musicals came from lighter versions of opera, like opéra comique and operetta (see p. 13). Towards the end of the 19th century, Gilbert and Sullivan wrote lots of comic operas that were really popular.

2) The type of musicals that are around today started in the 1920s, and developed throughout the rest of the 20th and into the 21st century. They started out on Broadway, a famous theatre street in New York. Some started in London's West End.

3) Musicals use singing, dancing and talking to tell stories.

4) They usually have an orchestra to accompany the singers and play incidental music (background music).

5) Some musicals that started out on the stage have been made into really popular films — like 'Grease', 'West Side Story' and 'Sweeney Todd'. Sometimes, a musical that started life as a film is adapted into a musical performed on stage — like 'Billy Elliot'.

6) Some musicals are based on novels — like 'Wicked' and 'Oliver!'.

Musical styles are always Changing

Musicals are generally written in the style of the popular music that's around at the time — so musicals from different times sound very different. Earlier musicals were influenced by jazz and swing music (see p. 42-43), while lots of musicals from the 1970s onwards used rock music (see p. 46).
Have a listen to some of these musicals to hear the different styles they use:

1920s-1950s	COLE PORTER	'Paris', 'Anything Goes', 'Kiss Me, Kate', 'Silk Stockings'
1940s-1950s	RODGERS & HAMMERSTEIN	'Oklahoma!', 'South Pacific', 'The King and I', 'The Sound of Music'
1950s-2000s	STEPHEN SONDHEIM	'Follies', 'Sweeney Todd' and lyrics for 'West Side Story'
1960s-1990s	KANDER & EBB	'Cabaret', 'Chicago', 'Kiss of the Spider Woman'
1970s-2000s	ANDREW LLOYD WEBBER	'Joseph and the Amazing Technicolour Dreamcoat', 'Jesus Christ Superstar', 'Evita', 'Cats', 'Phantom of the Opera'
1970s-2000s	SCHÖNBERG & BOUBLIL	'Les Miserables', 'Miss Saigon'

Some Pop Songs start life in Musicals...

Songs from musicals sometimes hit the charts. In the UK, musicals by Andrew Lloyd Webber and Tim Rice have spawned a few chart hits:

* *Don't Cry For Me Argentina* from 'Evita'.
* *Memory* from 'Cats'.
* *No Matter What* from 'Whistle Down the Wind' (sung by Boyzone).

...while some Musicals are made up of Pop Songs

On the other hand, sometimes chart hits find their way into musicals — 'Mamma Mia!' was written around a collection of Abba hits, and 'We Will Rock You' is based on the songs of Queen. The plots of these musicals often have nothing to do with the band, but use their songs to tell the story.

Songs from Musicals

Musicals need to show the <u>emotions</u> of the characters and <u>explain</u> what's happening in the story.

Most musical songs are Easy on the Ear

1) The tunes are easy to <u>sing</u> — audiences tend to prefer songs they can sing along to.

2) The harmony (the chords and stuff) is <u>diatonic</u> — all the notes are generally from a major or a minor scale.

3) The song <u>structure</u> is often <u>simple</u>, with alternating verses and choruses and a <u>middle eight</u>.

> INTRO   CHORUS   VERSE   CHORUS   VERSE   CHORUS   MIDDLE 8   VERSE   CHORUS   VERSE   CHORUS   OUTRO

Grabs the audience's attention and sets the mood for the song.

Has new chords and new lyrics. A change of mood to keep the audience interested.

Finishes the song off — either loud and brassy or sad and quiet.

4) The chorus is often in <u>32-bar song</u> form. The 32 bars break down into 4 sections of 8 bars each. Sections 1, 2 and 4 use the <u>main theme</u> (sometimes with slight variations). Section 3 has a <u>contrasting theme</u> (middle eight). The <u>structure</u>'s very similar to the structure of a <u>pop song</u>.

5) The chorus has a <u>hook</u> — a catchy nugget of lyrics and tune that makes the song memorable, e.g. *I like to be in America* ('West Side Story'), *Supercalifragilisticexpialidocious* ('Mary Poppins') or *And all that jazz* ('Chicago'). The hook is the bit that gets stuck in the audience's head (so they can't help ordering a CD when they get home) and often becomes the title of the song.

oops

There are Four Basic Types of musical song

1) *SOLO CHARACTER SONG* — a character sings about how they're <u>feeling</u> — in love, full of hate, over the moon with happiness, etc. *Memory* from 'Cats' and *Something's Coming* from 'West Side Story' are both solo character songs.

2) *DUET* — duets are basically the same as solo character songs, except there are <u>two people</u> singing so you get two different reactions to a situation. *I Know Him So Well* from 'Chess' and *Sixteen Going on Seventeen* from 'The Sound of Music' are both good examples.

3) *ACTION SONG* — the words of the song tell you what's going on in the <u>plot</u> — they lead you into the next bit of the story.

4) *CHORUS NUMBER* — the whole cast get together and have a big old sing-song. Like at the end of *Grease* — 'We go together like ramma lamma lamma ka dingedy ding de dong...' and *You Can't Stop the Beat* at the end of 'Hairspray'.

All these styles of song developed from opera — solo songs are like <u>arias</u> and action songs are like <u>recitatives</u> (see p. 13).

The <u>lyrics</u> in a musical song tell part of the story. They're usually <u>written first</u> — the composer has to fit the music around them.

Hopelessly devoted — to revision...

Musicals have been pushed into the public view recently, what with TV reality programmes like 'How Do You Solve a Problem Like Maria?' and 'Any Dream Will Do'. Makes you wonder what they're going to do next — 'There Are Worse Things I Could Do'? Or maybe 'Past the Point of No Return'? Hmmm...

Leonard Bernstein — Something's Coming

Not all musicals are happy and light-hearted. 'West Side Story' is quite dark and has a sad ending.

Leonard Bernstein wrote 'West Side Story'

1) Leonard Bernstein was born in Massachusetts in 1918. He was an award-winning composer and conductor, as well as a teacher and author. He died in 1990.
2) He studied Music at Harvard University, and later studied piano, conducting, orchestration and counterpoint in Philadelphia.
3) He was one of America's most internationally respected musicians. Some of the recordings he made when conducting the New York Philharmonic Orchestra are still considered to be among the best around.
4) 'West Side Story' is one of his best known works. He wrote it in 1957 and it's still performed today.
5) Bernstein also wrote another four musicals, three symphonies, two operas, an operetta and lots of chamber music. He also composed the music for the 1954 film *On The Waterfront*.

'West Side Story' is a Musical

1) 'West Side Story' is set in New York in the 1950s. It's about two rival gangs, the Jets (Americans) and the Sharks (Puerto Rican immigrants).
2) It follows the tragic love story of Tony, the best friend of the Jets' leader and Maria, the sister of the Sharks' leader.
3) The story's quite similar to 'Romeo and Juliet', though there are some differences — the main one is that Maria (Juliet) doesn't die at the end. Tony (Romeo) does though.
4) It has two acts, with spoken dialogue between the songs. There are solos, duets and action songs. It also has a lot of numbers that are just danced to.
5) 'West Side Story' is a collaboration between Bernstein, Jerome Robbins (the director and choreographer who came up with the idea), Arthur Laurents (the scriptwriter) and Stephen Sondheim (the lyricist).
6) It was quite different to other musicals at the time — it had a sad ending, lots of dance scenes and looked at social problems in America.

It's written for a Big Orchestra

1) Lots of Broadway musicals from the 1950s need a big orchestra — and 'West Side Story' definitely does. It needs players who can double up — play more than one instrument (although not at the same time).
2) The orchestra includes saxophones, piano, electric guitar, mandolin and celeste — as well as the usual wind, brass and string sections. Even these sections were large. It also uses a lot of percussion, including timpani, a glockenspiel and a police whistle.
3) Tony is sung by a tenor (a high male voice), while Maria is sung by a soprano (a high female voice).
4) Bernstein uses Latin American rhythms and instruments (like castanets, a güiro and maracas) to reflect the background of the Puerto Rican gang.
5) He also uses lots of jazz elements — like blue notes and syncopation (see p. 40).
6) There are lots of well known songs in 'West Side Story' — like *Tonight*, *America*, *I Feel Pretty* and *Somewhere*. The one you need to know about for your exam is *Something's Coming*.

Two street gangs — both alike in dignity...

Songs from *West Side Story* have been used in lots of films, TV programmes and adverts. You might have heard them in *The Simpsons*™ or *Friends*. Some programmes take the mickey out of the songs and dances.

Leonard Bernstein — Something's Coming

Something's coming — yes, another lovely page on 'West Side Story'. Relax, enjoy and learn.

Something's Coming is sung by Tony

1) *Something's Coming* comes quite early in the show. It's a solo for Tony — he's imagining a better future for himself. He sings it before he meets Maria.
2) He's excited about the future — you can hear the excitement in the music.
3) The lyrics talk about a 'miracle' coming — this could be meeting Maria. It's dramatic irony, as meeting her leads to his death. 'Something's coming' isn't necessarily 'something good'.

The piece has lots of Cross Rhythms

1) The song's written in 3/4, but sometimes it feels like it's in 6/8 — in the piano part, the left hand plays three crotchets while the right hand plays quavers as if it's in 6/8. The quavers have accents on the first and fourth quavers in the bar — it makes it feel like two dotted crotchet beats in a bar (rather than the three crotchets of 3/4).
2) Lots of the parts are playing cross-rhythms (see p. 64).
3) Much of Tony's part feels like it's in 6/8 — with two beats in a bar. The accented off-beats (like in his first two entries — 'could be' and 'who knows') give a sense of anticipation, which matches his mood.
4) It's a fast song — it's marked ♩ = 176. The quick tempo reflects Tony's excitement.
5) At the start, Tony sings pianissimo (*pp*) in a half-whispering style, with quaver rests between words. This gives it a breathless, agitated feeling — he's impatient to leave the gang behind.
6) *Something's Coming*'s in D major. Major keys are often used to reflect happy emotions — at this point, Tony's excited and looking forward to the future.
7) The final word 'tonight' is echoed later on in the song *Tonight* that he sings with Maria.
8) There are ostinati (repeated patterns — ostinati is the plural of ostinato) in lots of parts. Listen out for the three crotchets in the bass parts and the accented quaver pattern in some other parts. There's imitation between instruments too.

Bernstein uses Tritones in 'West Side Story'

1) A tritone is an interval of two notes that are three whole tones apart (like F to B). In Medieval music they were known as the 'diabolus in musica' (the 'devil in music') and composers were banned from using them in church music.

2) Even today, composers often use tritones when something is evil or scary — in the film *Psycho*, a shrill tritone accompanies each stab of the knife in the infamous shower scene.
3) Tritones appear in several places in 'West Side Story', showing that underneath the love story something bad is happening. There's a tritone in the first chord of *Something's Coming* — the D and the G♯ in the piano part give it an edgy, unpredictable feeling.

4) They're often used as an appoggiatura (see p. 12) — that's how Bernstein's used it here.

Tonight, tonight — lots of revision to be done tonight...

'Something's coming, something good' — ah, so full of hope. That's just asking for trouble. It's up there with 'nothing can possibly go wrong' and 'no more lies'. You just know something bad's going to happen.

Revision Summary

Poor old Tony, he doesn't have an easy time of things, what with all the fighting, heartache and jazz hands flying around — but at least he didn't have to worry about his GCSE Music exam on top of everything else. Don't go thinking this stuff's all dead easy just because it's not really really old — you need to be able to talk about the features of expressionism, minimalism and songs from musicals in your exam.

1) What are the rough dates of the Romantic period?
2) What are chromatic notes?
3) What is atonal music? How did it affect traditional musical forms?
4) Why did Schoenberg choose to write atonal music instead of tonal music?
5) Write down five features of expressionist music.
6) When did Schoenberg write 'Five Orchestral Pieces'?
7) What does the word *Peripetie* mean in English?
8) What ensemble is *Peripetie* written for?
9) Explain what is meant by hexachord and complement.
10) What does 'tone-colour melody' mean and why does Schoenberg use it in *Peripetie*?
11) What are the three ways that the Prime Order of a piece can be rearranged?
12) When was minimalism developed?
13) Minimalist music is often made up of loops. What are loops?
14) Write down four different ways of changing the loop patterns in minimalist music.
15) Give two ways that music from other countries influenced minimalist music.
16) When did Steve Reich write 'Electric Counterpoint'?
17) What instruments play the 3rd Movement from 'Electric Counterpoint'?
18) Explain the process of looping to build up layers used in the 3rd Movement from 'Electric Counterpoint'.
19) What is polyphonic texture?
20) Which two keys are used in the 3rd Movement from 'Electric Counterpoint'?
21) Which two time signatures are used in the 3rd Movement from 'Electric Counterpoint'? What time signature is the main part of the piece written in?
22) What does diatonic mean?
23) What is the structure of the 32-bar song form?
24) What is a hook (in the context of musical song lyrics not the captain)?
25) What are the four basic types of musical song?
26) When did Leonard Bernstein write 'West Side Story'?
27) Write down the simple plot of 'West Side Story'.
28) What kind of voice is Tony's part written for?
29) What is Tony singing about in *Something's Coming*?
30) What is the effect of the pianissimo (*pp*) at the beginning of *Something's Coming*?
31) What time signature is used in *Something's Coming*? What time signature does it sometimes feel like and why?
32) What key is used in *Something's Coming*?
33) What is a tritone, and why does Bernstein use it in *Something's Coming*?

The Blues

Like most music, blues gets a lot of its flavour from the scales it uses.

African Slaves in America started off the Blues

Blues is a combination of African and European musical styles. It first started on the slave plantations of the southern United States in the nineteenth century.

1) In the 1600s and 1700s hundreds of thousands of Africans were captured and sold as slaves. They were taken to work on plantations in North America.

2) To pass the time and take their minds off the work, which was often brutally hard, they sang worksongs — the beat of the songs matched the rhythm of the work. The lyrics were often about the hardship and misery of living as a slave.

3) Over the years, African musical styles like call and response singing blended with features of European music, especially chords. This combination was the beginning of the blues.

4) Even after slavery was finally abolished in the 1860s, ex-slaves living in the southern states were poor and powerless. The lyrics and tone of their songs carried on being sad and 'blue'.

5) The traditional blues instruments are harmonica, guitar, banjo, violin, piano, double bass and the voice. They're all acoustic — electric instruments hadn't been invented when blues began.

6) In the early twentieth century black Americans started playing the blues in bars and clubs beyond the southern states. By the 1920s blues was massively popular all over America with white and black audiences.

Blues has its Own Scale

1) You get a blues scale by flattening the third and seventh of any major scale by a semitone. The fifth note's sometimes flattened too.

2) The flattened notes are known as the blue notes.

3) The blue notes are notes that were 'bent' in African singing. The singers would 'slide' up or down to a note, giving it a twang and making it slightly flatter.

4) The second and sixth notes are often left out.

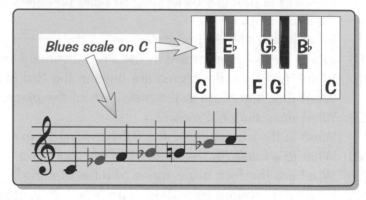

Blues scale on C

Blues melodies have Swinging Off-beat Rhythms

1) In normal 'straight' rhythm the beats split up into equal halves.

I want chips and egg

I want chips and egg

2) In the blues, the first bit of the beat nicks some time from the second bit. The first bit ends up longer and with more oomph. This gives the music a swinging feel.

3) The blues uses lots of syncopation (see p. 43). You get a lively off-beat sound by avoiding the strong beats — it puts the oomph in unexpected places.

Please don't make me beg

The Blues — 12 Bar Blues

There are lots of different types of blues, but the most popular song structure is the 12-bar blues.
Ladies and gentlemen — let's hear a big hand for... the 12-bar blues...

12-bar Blues repeats a twelve-bar structure

12-bar blues is a set chord pattern, twelve bars long. Singers like Bessie Smith and
Robert Johnson made the 12-bar blues structure really popular in the 1920s — it's been
around ever since and is still one of the most popular styles.

BAR 1	BAR 2	BAR 3	BAR 4
Chord I	Chord I	Chord I	Chord I

BAR 5	BAR 6	BAR 7	BAR 8
Chord IV	Chord IV	Chord I	Chord I

BAR 9	BAR 10	BAR 11	BAR 12
Chord V	Chord IV	Chord I	Chord I

To lead back into bar 1
you play chord V in bar 12
instead of chord I.

1) The only chords are I, IV and V.
   (See Section Four of the Core Book.)

2) The twelve-bar pattern's repeated right through the song.

3) You can make the chords even more bluesy by adding the minor 7ths (see Section Four of the Core Book).

> 12-bar blues has had a huge influence on other musical styles including ragtime, jazz, rock'n'roll, country & western and R&B. Some pop songs today still use the standard 12-bar structure.

Twelve Bars breaks nicely into Three Lines

The twelve-bar chord pattern of 12-bar blues breaks up nicely into three lines, each with four bars.
The lyrics of a 12-bar blues song usually stick to three lines for each verse of the song.

Lines 1 and 2 are usually the same.

Line 3 is different, but rhymes with lines 1 and 2.

> Woke up this morning feeling blue.
> Woke up this morning feeling blue.
> Feeling sad and lonesome without you.

The words are usually pretty gloomy.

Each line takes up 4 bars, but the words don't always fill up the whole line.
The singer's bit — the call — is followed by an instrument playing an
answer — the response — in the gap before the next line.

You can have any colour you like so long as it's blue...

The blues doesn't have to be mournful, sad and depressing — it just sounds better that way... If you
fancy writing a blues piece for one of your compositions, remember to use all the things that make the
blues sound like the blues — blue notes, swinging rhythm, three-line verses and call and response.

Jazz

Jazz is a pretty massive subject, so I've tried to cram the important bits into these two pages.
You'll probably have heard lots of jazz — it's a word used to cover quite a few types of music.

Jazz has its Roots in African American Blues and Ragtime

1) Jazz is a type of music that developed in the USA in the early 20th century. It's a fusion of African and European influences that came from the music of the newly-freed slaves.

2) It started off as Dixieland jazz in New Orleans in the early 1900s. Dixieland jazz is a mix of brass band marches, ragtime (music with lots of syncopated melodies that was often played on the piano) and blues (see p. 40-41). Dixieland jazz is polyphonic (different parts move at different times). It was played in brothels and bars — the only places black musicians were allowed to perform because of segregation (black people weren't allowed to use the same places as white people, like schools and bars).

3) In 1920, jazz moved to Chicago. This was the era of the Prohibition (from 1920-1933, alcohol was banned in the United States). Illegal bars (called speakeasies) often had jazz bands playing. Jazz started to get a bad reputation. Some people thought it was immoral.

4) The 1920s were known as 'The Jazz Age' or the 'Roaring Twenties'.

Swing Music was popular in the 1930s and 40s

1) Swing music is a type of jazz that can be danced to. It's more structured than Dixieland jazz.

2) It's usually quite fast, and rhythms are swung (see p. 40). Most pieces are in 4/4. It was meant to be danced to, so it had regular phrases and emphasis on the first and third beats of the bar.

3) Swing is played by a big band (see p.43).

4) It was popular because it was played on the radio — it was a lot more accessible and acceptable than going to the brothels and illegal bars.

5) During the Second World War, swing became less popular because lots of the men who played in the big bands had gone off to war.

6) After the war, bebop (or just bop) developed from swing music. Bebop was fast with lots of improvisation. It had complex harmonies, exciting syncopated rhythms, and irregular phrase lengths. Bebop was much less structured than swing.

Free Jazz broke all the Rules

1) Free jazz is a type of jazz that developed in the 1950s and 60s. It was a reaction against the limits of swing and bebop.

2) It didn't follow the normal rules of tempo and rhythm — players within the same band would play at different speeds to each other. There wasn't a regular rhythm.

3) There was lots of improvisation — the soloist didn't follow the chords or structure of the rest of the band.

4) Jazz didn't stop developing in the 60s. In the 60s and 70s new types emerged, like soul jazz, Latin jazz and jazz fusion. Since then, there's been experimental jazz and fusions of jazz with other types of music.

All in a flap...

In the Jazz Age, young women started wearing shorter skirts and cutting their hair into bobs. They listened to jazz music, smoked and drove cars (gasp). They were called 'flappers' and I want to be one.

Jazz

Jazz has lots of features that make it <u>easy to recognise</u>. You know it when you hear it — it has a <u>swing</u> to it.

Trumpets, Trombones and Clarinets are jazz instruments

1) A typical <u>jazz band</u> would have a <u>trumpet</u>, a <u>trombone</u> and a <u>clarinet</u> on the <u>front row</u>. Later, <u>saxophones</u> were included too. The <u>front row instruments</u> play <u>improvised solos</u>.

2) There'd be a <u>rhythm section</u> with <u>piano</u>, <u>guitar</u>, <u>drums</u> and a <u>double bass</u>.

3) Big bands are made up of <u>saxophones</u>, <u>trumpets</u>, <u>trombones</u> and a <u>rhythm section</u>. The sax section has <u>alto</u>, <u>tenor</u> and <u>baritone saxophones</u> and sometimes <u>clarinets</u>. Some big bands have a <u>singer</u> too.

4) A typical big band would have <u>5 saxophone</u> (2 altos, 2 tenors and a baritone), <u>4 trumpets</u>, <u>4 trombones</u> and a <u>4-piece rhythm section</u> (piano, bass, guitar and drums).

Jazz is Swung and Syncopated

1) Early jazz music was based on a <u>12-bar blues</u> (see p. 41).

2) The <u>chords</u> were played by the <u>rhythm section</u> and the <u>front row</u> instruments would <u>improvise</u> over them.

3) Jazz musicians use <u>call and response</u> and <u>blue notes</u> — key features of jazz and blues. Blue notes are <u>flattened 3rds</u>, <u>7ths</u> and sometimes <u>5ths</u> of a <u>major scale</u>.

4) <u>Syncopated rhythms</u> move the strong beat away from the first and third beats of the bar. <u>Swung rhythms</u> (see p. 40) are also used.

5) Some musicians use <u>scat</u> — a type of <u>improvised singing</u> with <u>nonsense words</u> and <u>syllables</u>.

Jazz has lots of Improvisation

1) <u>Improvisation</u> is a really important feature of jazz. It's when a soloist <u>makes up</u> music <u>on the spot</u>.

2) If the band's playing a <u>12-bar blues</u>, the soloist knows which notes fit over the chords. The <u>pianist</u> or <u>guitarist</u> supports the soloist by <u>comping</u> — playing chords under the solo.

3) <u>Improvisations</u> are <u>different</u> every time.

4) The <u>improvised</u> nature of jazz means the same piece can be played in radically <u>different</u> ways — depending on the <u>interpretation</u> of it. Even if a piece is played twice by the same people, it <u>won't</u> sound the same.

5) <u>Swing music</u> has <u>less</u> improvisation — people wanted tunes they could <u>recognise</u>. There are still some sections for a soloist to improvise over, but they're <u>shorter</u>.

6) Jazz <u>songs</u> are a bit different — the singer has <u>less chance</u> to improvise (but they can use <u>scat</u>).

Jazz music Wasn't Written Down

1) In early jazz (and in some today), the music <u>wasn't written down</u>.

2) There was lots of <u>interaction</u> between the soloist and the band, like <u>call and response</u> — the soloist would play a phrase (the <u>call</u>) and the band would answer it (the <u>response</u>) or the other way around. Sometimes the soloist would <u>repeat</u> ideas heard earlier in the piece and <u>develop</u> them in the solo.

3) The band would follow the <u>band leader</u>. Sometimes the band leader would also be the <u>soloist</u> or the <u>composer</u> — like <u>Louis Armstrong</u>, <u>Duke Ellington</u> and <u>Glenn Miller</u>.

4) Popular jazz pieces are called <u>jazz standards</u>. They're pieces that are part of a band's <u>repertoire</u>. Some jazz standards are '<u>I Got Rhythm</u>', '<u>My Funny Valentine</u>' and '<u>Take The "A" Train</u>'.

Jazz — anything goes...

Phew. Jazz is a pretty huge topic — I could write a whole book about it. This page tells you about some of its key features. You'll hear a lot of these in Miles Davis' *All Blues*, which is what the next two pages are about.

Miles Davis — All Blues

All Blues is from the album '<u>Kind of Blue</u>' which was released in <u>1959</u>. It still sells about <u>125,000</u> copies a year.

Miles Davis changed the way jazz was played

1) Miles Davis was born in <u>1926</u> in <u>Illinois</u>, <u>America</u> and died in <u>1991</u>. He started playing the <u>trumpet</u> when he was a young boy, and went on to become a <u>band leader</u> and <u>composer</u> as well.

2) In the <u>1940s</u>, Miles was getting fed up of <u>bebop</u> (see p. 42). He didn't like the <u>constantly changing chords</u> that the <u>improvised solos</u> were based on, so he started composing music using <u>fewer chords</u>. The slower harmonic rhythm meant the soloist could <u>develop</u> their <u>melody</u> more before the chords changed.

3) Miles' solos <u>changed</u> the way jazz was played. He used to:

- improvise using a <u>tuneful melody</u> (that you could sing along to) rather than lots of <u>crazy runs</u>.
- play very <u>lyrically</u> — as though he was <u>singing</u>.
- base his improvisations on <u>scales</u> (or sometimes modes) and an <u>overall key signature</u>, rather than <u>chord changes</u> every <u>bar</u>.
- make the trumpet sound <u>natural</u> and <u>pure</u> (not <u>forced</u> and <u>high-pitched</u>).
- often play in the <u>lower register</u>.

4) Miles was capable of playing <u>technically demanding</u> music, but he preferred a <u>simpler</u> approach.

5) The whole of '<u>Kind of Blue</u>' was based on <u>scales</u> rather than <u>chords</u>. It let the musicians <u>improvise freely</u>.

All Blues was recorded in One Take

In *All Blues*, the performers <u>improvised</u> on <u>basic scales</u>. The <u>key features</u> of this piece are:

1) PITCH — all instruments keep to their <u>middle</u> and <u>lower registers</u>.

2) DURATION — *All Blues* lasts for more than <u>11 and a half</u> minutes.

3) DYNAMICS — the piece is generally quite <u>subdued</u> — most of it's <u>moderately loud</u> (*mf*), except for a few louder trumpet bits. The <u>ensemble</u> plays even more <u>quietly</u> when a <u>soloist</u> is playing.

4) TEMPO — it's marked '<u>jazz waltz</u>' — it should be played at a <u>moderate pace</u>.

5) TIME SIGNATURE — unlike most jazz and blues at the time, *All Blues* is in <u>6/4</u> (6 crotchets in a bar).

6) TIMBRE — the timbre's very <u>mellow</u> (the timbre's the overall <u>sound</u> of the piece). Miles uses a <u>mute</u>, <u>ghost notes</u> (notes that are <u>hinted</u> at, rather than <u>played</u> — they're deliberately <u>weak</u> beats) and <u>rests</u> in his solos to make it more mellow.

7) TEXTURE — it has a <u>simple</u> texture — the <u>wind instruments</u> play in 3rds and 4ths, while the <u>piano</u> and <u>double bass</u> play a <u>simple riff</u> and <u>chords</u>. The <u>drum</u> keeps a <u>steady beat</u>.

8) STRUCTURE — *All Blues* uses a standard <u>12-bar blues</u> chord pattern (see p. 41) in G which gets <u>repeated</u> throughout the piece. It's played under the <u>solos</u> and the <u>main melody</u>. The chords <u>aren't</u> exactly the same as the traditional 12-bar blues though — they're a bit <u>fancier</u>:

Bar of 12-Bar Blues	1	2	3	4	5	6	7	8	9	10	11	12
Traditional Chords	I	I	I	I	IV	IV	1	1	V	IV	1	1
All Blues Chords	I⁷	I⁷	I⁷	I⁷	IV⁷	IV⁷	I⁷	I⁷	V⁷#⁹	VI♭⁷#⁹ V⁷#⁹	I⁷	I⁷

#9 means there's an <u>augmented 9th</u> in there — that's a <u>2nd</u>, but <u>up</u> an octave and <u>raised</u> by a <u>semitone</u>. Phew.

Miles to go — well, one more page on this piece...

Make sure you know the <u>key features</u> of *All Blues* — and how it was <u>different</u> to the type of jazz that came before it. Learn the <u>chord pattern</u> too — you might have to fill in some <u>missing chords</u> in your exam.

Miles Davis — All Blues

Miles Davis believed that 'less is more' when it came to solos. He made them very lyrical.

All Blues is mainly Improvised

1) The band's made up of a trumpet, alto saxophone, tenor saxophone, piano, double bass and drums.
2) The trumpet, both saxophones and the piano each have an improvised solo. The two saxes tend to play together when they're not playing solos.
3) When they turned up to the recording session, the band had very little idea what they were going to play. Miles gave them a few scales and melody lines to improvise on. He also gave them brief instructions, then off they went.
4) The whole album was recorded in two sessions, and each piece was recorded in one take.

The piece is divided into Sections

1) *All Blues* has an intro, followed by the head (theme). There are four improvised solos, then the head returns.
2) The drums keep time and the piano plays chords or tremolo chords (except for its improvised solo).
3) The double bass plays Riff A from bar 9 onwards (for most of the piece).
4) The piece finishes with a final coda which fades out.
   A riff is a modern word for an ostinato — a repeated pattern.
   It can be in the melody, rhythm or chord pattern.

1) INTRO

The intro is 8 bars long. It's made up of two four-bar sections (called Intro 1 and Intro 2). In Intro 2, the alto and tenor saxes play Riff B in 3rds (they don't play anything in the first four bars).

2) HEAD (32 BARS)

The head lasts for 32 bars. A muted trumpet plays a 12-bar theme (the saxes play Riff B in the background). They play Intro 2 followed by the theme again, followed by another repetition of Intro 2.

3) IMPROVISED SOLO SECTIONS

The four solo sections each feature a different instrument — first it's the trumpet, followed by the alto sax, then the tenor sax and finally the piano. All the solos are improvised. The trumpet solo and both saxophone solos last for 48 bars and the piano solo lasts for 24. After each of the solos, Intro 2 is played (but the piano plays Riff B instead of the saxes — except after the piano solo, when the saxes play it again).

4) HEAD (32 BARS)

The head comes back again — it's the 12-bar theme followed by Intro 2. They play both bits twice.

5) OUTRO

All Blues finishes with a 12-bar outro which fades out. The saxophones are playing Riff B again, but the trumpet introduces a new riff, Riff C.

Ghost notes (see p. 44)

I'm blue — da ba dee da ba dow...

This page looks a bit scary, but don't worry — it's not as bad as it looks. Most of the sections of *All Blues* are quite similar, so you just have to know what's different in each section. Listen out for the riffs too.

Rock Music

Rock stars must have a pretty nice life, what with the posh hotels, adoring fans and truckloads of money. But it's their music that made them famous, and that's what this page is about.

Rock Music's based on the 12-Bar Blues

1) Rock music started off in the 1950s. The chord structure's based on the 12-bar blues (see p. 41).
2) A rock band was originally made up of a lead electric guitar, a rhythm electric guitar, a lead singer, a bass guitar and a drummer.
3) As rock developed, more instruments were added. Some bands introduced a string section (with violins and cellos), some had brass sections (trumpets and trombones) and some had wind sections (flutes, clarinets, saxophones and oboes). They also brought in keyboards and synthesizers.
4) Musicians used the effects on electric guitars to produce new sounds — like distortion, feedback (the noise you get when you stand too close to a speaker with a guitar or microphone) and reverberation (echo).
5) Rock bands use lots of other techniques to get unusual sounds — the band Led Zeppelin used a pounding beat turned up really loud as their main rhythm. They sometimes used violin bows on their guitar strings to get a sustained note.

In the 1970s, rock songs started to Develop

1) Bands in the 1970s started to develop the basic rock formula to make their songs last longer. Their songs had themes and some even told stories.
2) Queen's 'Bohemian Rhapsody' lasts for a whopping 6 minutes. It doesn't have a chorus — it's made up of unrelated sections, including a slow ballad, a guitar solo, an operatic section and a heavy rock section.
3) Pink Floyd's 1973 album 'The Dark Side of the Moon' is a concept album — there's a theme that links all the tracks.

Rock songs became a way of Expressing Yourself

1) Lots of rock bands write their own lyrics to songs (as well as the music). They use things like religious themes, protest songs and personal experiences of love.
2) Led Zeppelin, David Bowie and Bob Dylan all use the influences of folk music — they've written whole albums in a folky style.
3) Bob Dylan is also famous for his protest songs — his folky 'Blowin' In The Wind' is used as an anti-war song.
4) The more rock developed, the fewer rules it followed. Songs could be any length, and follow any chord pattern (or none at all). Bands could have any instruments, and the lyrics could be about whatever the band wanted.
5) Even costumes were used to help the music along — David Bowie's silver suit and lightning make-up really helped to set the scene for Major Tom (an astronaut who is in a lot of Bowie's songs).

Powerful Guitars were important in 1990s Rock

1) A lot of rock bands in the 1990s were guitar-based — they used guitars to create a really powerful sound. Power chords (made up of the tonic and fifth of a chord) were used a lot.
2) Bands like Nirvana, Green Day and Pearl Jam were really popular. They wrote songs about controversial topics (like drugs and mental illness) and often swore a lot.
3) 1990s rock music was fused with other types of music — like grunge, punk and funk.

Don't stop me now...

Well, another page bites the dust. It's just a crazy little thing called revision. I know you're under pressure, but you're about half-way through this section, then there's only one more to go before you can break free.

Jeff Buckley — Grace

Jeff Buckley only actually released one studio album — he died before his second was completed.

'Grace' was Jeff Buckley's Debut Album

1) Jeff Buckley was born in California in 1966. He was a singer-songwriter and guitarist.
   He became popular in the early 1990s.
2) His early work was influenced by Led Zeppelin and Kiss, two of his favourite bands.
   He also performed covers of songs by Led Zeppelin, Bob Dylan and Elton John.
3) He released one studio album, 'Grace', in 1994, and was working on a second when he died in 1997 —
   he drowned whilst swimming in a river. The second album was released in 1998, a year after his death.

   - The album 'Grace' includes seven original songs and three covers.
   - When it was first released, sales were pretty poor (even though the critics liked it).
     Since then, it's gone on to sell really well — it's now sold over 2 million copies.
   - You need to know about the song Grace, an original song written by Jeff Buckley and Gary Lucas.
   - Grace is about Buckley moving from L.A. to New York to be with someone he loved.
     He's not afraid of what lies ahead because he's in love.

Grace has a Folk-Rock Feel

1) Grace has a wide vocal range — at some points, Buckley sings falsetto (higher than the normal male range).
   He also uses vibrato and scoops up to notes (he starts a note lower then slides up to the written note —
   this is also called portamento).
2) The piece starts quietly, with just two electric guitars playing (one distorted and one not). There's also
   an eerie wailing in the background played by a synthesizer (see p. 48).
3) The dynamics are increased by bringing in more instruments — after a few bars, the bass guitar and drums
   come in. By the end, there's a full rock band playing, with heavy drums, screaming vocals and wailing
   guitars. The instruments don't actually get louder themselves, but more are added to make it more intense.
4) It's in a steady 12/8, with four dotted crotchet beats in a bar. This is quite unusual — most rock songs
   are in 4/4. It feels faster though, as the guitar plays semiquaver runs at the beginning.
5) It has a fairly typical verse-chorus structure, with a guitar solo towards the end. The intro is repeated
   after the choruses, and the piece ends with a short outro.
6) There are four main guitar riffs (see p. 45) in the piece. The first riff's made up of semiquavers and it's
   played by the electric guitar in the introduction, then repeated between verses. The electric guitar plays
   another riff in the verses — this one's made up of broken chords (the notes of the chord,
   but played separately). The acoustic guitar plays a rhythmic, percussive riff in the
   verses and choruses. In the final section of the piece, both guitars play a fourth riff,
   while the vocals build to a screaming climax. The riffs build up the texture of the piece.
7) There are some electronic effects used in the piece — like EQ and delay (see p. 49).
   They also use a flanger to create a swirly sound (flangers are added in a studio).
8) Buckley used unusual chord progressions — he chose chords that he liked the sound of.
   The main part of Grace is in E minor.
9) Considering this song's supposed to be about love, the lyrics are surprisingly morbid.
   The line 'wait in the fire' is repeated again and again, and it's followed by 'burn'. Hardly romantic.

Buckley's other works are also Popular

1) Lots of the other songs on the album were really popular. 'Grace' included a cover of Leonard Cohen's
   Hallelujah, as well as Lilac Wine and Benjamin Britten's Corpus Christi Carol.
2) His second studio album (released after his death) was called 'Sketches for My Sweetheart the Drunk'.
3) He also released quite a few live albums — like 'Live at Sin-é' (1993) and 'Live from the Bataclan' (1995).

Burn, baby, burn...

I don't think I'd like someone to write a song like this about me. To me, it doesn't so much say 'hearts and
flowers', more 'fire and death'. Not what I'm looking for. A nice bouquet of flowers would be much better.

Dance/Electronic Music

Electronic music is any music that uses electrical devices or instruments to produce and alter the sounds used in the music. Most club dance music has electronic influences.

Lots of Twentieth Century Music uses electronic instruments

Electronic devices and instruments were used by composers in the twentieth century and are still used today.

In the 1920s, the idea of 'futuristic music' really took off. Darius Milhaud was the first composer to use sampling (see p.49) in his work. He experimented with changing the speeds of vocal recordings. A composer called Ottorino Respighi used a recording of a nightingale in his orchestral composition *Pini di Roma* (*Pines of Rome*). Another composer, George Antheil, composed a piece for pianos, xylophones, pianola (a self-playing piano), doorbells and an aeroplane propeller.

In the 1940s, music that used non-musical or man-made sounds (like car doors slamming, car horns, hitting car bonnets, bird songs etc.) was known as 'Musique Concrète'.
The sounds were recorded onto tapes then manipulated in different ways, for example:
- Playing them at different speeds.
- Cutting up the tape and putting it back together in a different order.
- Looping (recording a short section on to a tape, then making a loop of the tape to play it over and over again).

Electronic Dance Music is played in Clubs

1) Most dance music today is created by electronic devices. There are lots of different types of electronic dance music and they're all slightly different.
2) The different types can be quite hard to define — there are so many sub-groups, and lots of bands play more than one type. The name 'club dance music' covers things like house, techno, trance and ambient.

Synthesizers and Sequencers are used to Create music

1) The main development in electronic music happened in the 1960s, when Robert Moog and Herbert Deutsch produced the voltage-controlled synthesizer. A synthesizer is an electronic device used to produce sounds.
2) Synthesizers are usually controlled by a keyboard (a piano keyboard rather than a computer keyboard), with buttons and slides to create different effects.
3) Lots of music can be produced just using a laptop — you can even download a virtual synthesizer.
4) A sequencer is a piece of computer software. It's a MIDI recording and playback device (MIDI stands for Musical Instrument Digital Interface — every note, instrument sound, key signature, tempo and any other musical direction is given a computer code. This means that different types of computers and recording equipment can 'talk' to each other). The sequencer tells a MIDI instrument to play notes in a certain way or particular order.
5) A sequencer doesn't actually record sound — it just uses MIDI information. This makes it easy to correct mistakes or change volume or timing.
6) A sequencer lets you make loops of short sections of sounds, which can be repeated and recorded to produce backing tracks. You can make loops of drumbeats, chords and even tunes. They're used a lot in electronic club dance music.
7) Cubase, Pro-Tools® and Logic Pro are sequencer programs that are widely used.

It was the nightingale — no, it was Ottorino Respighi...

'Musique Concrète' — ooo, think of the possibilities. You could sample washing machines spinning, phones ringing, waterfalls, printers, rainfall, the beeps of a till at the supermarket — I could go on for ages. I'm not entirely sure what the final piece would be like, but it'd be different, that's for sure.

Dance/Electronic Music

All the technology used in electronic music can get a bit confusing — you've got synthesizers and sequencers (covered on the previous page) and samplers too. You also need to know the different ways these electronic devices can change sounds and music.

Samplers are a bit like Synthesizers

Stevie Wonder used a digital sampler on his album 'The Secret Life of Plants'.

1) Samplers are another type of electronic equipment used to produce and alter music. They're a bit like synthesizers but they don't create the sounds themselves — they just play music back. The first digital sampler was invented in 1975.
2) Samples are short bits of recorded music. You can use samples of anything from live instruments to vinyl records. Samples can also be taken from a CD or MIDI track.
3) Samplers are told which samples to play by a sequencer or keyboard controller — the samples are assigned to a note on a keyboard and can be played, looped or recorded straight onto a track.
4) Samplers, synthesizers and sequencers mean that you don't have to be able to play any of the instruments you want to use in your recording, you can just use a computer program to get the sounds you want.

You can Change samples

You can use a virtual recording studio on your computer to alter and manipulate your samples.
These are some of the main ways that samples can be altered:

LOOPING	Uses a computer to loop music rather than doing it by hand — see p. 48.
PITCH SHIFTER	Plays the sample at different pitches.
PANNING	Changes which speaker the music comes out of.
CHORUS	Creates several layers of the sample — it sounds like there is more than one copy playing.
ECHO/DELAY	Adds echoes to the music — and even makes them in time with the beat.
REVERB	Changes the sample to make it sound as if it's being played in a large concert hall. (It can also take away all sound of reverb and make it feel flat.)
PHASER	Makes a 'whooshing' sound using the sample.
EQ	Short for equalization. It amplifies or removes frequencies (like bass or treble) — it can filter out frequencies above/below a certain level. Low-pass and high pass filters are both types of EQ.
LOW-PASS FILTER	Gets rid of 'noise' (like hissing or other background noises).
HIGH-PASS FILTER	'Cleans' the sample — it can get rid of low-pitched rumblings in the background.
DISTORTION	Changes the sound of a sample (it distorts it). Used as a guitar effect as well.

Some musicians use Samples in Live Performances

There are some musicians who use and manipulate samples live, using effects units like:
1) KAOSS — a DJ program that's connected to the decks and a laptop. You use your fingers on a touch screen to pull, bend and distort the music as it's playing.
2) SERATO (or SCRATCH LIVE) — a program that takes digital audio files and lets you create the DJ effect of scratching a vinyl record on a turntable. DJs like Fatboy Slim and Mark Ronson use it.

I'd like a sample of that cake please...

Don't be scared by all the technical stuff on this page — you don't need an in-depth understanding of how each bit works, you just need to know what they can do. Remember, a lot of dance music uses this equipment.

Electronica

Not to be confused with electronic music in general, Electronica is in a sub-category all of its own.

The Definition of Electronica has Changed over time

1) In the early 1990s, Electronica was used to describe all electronic music that used electronic instruments and sequencers or manipulated sounds electronically.

2) Towards the end of the 90s, it was used for bands and artists who made it really obvious that they were using electronic instruments and samples in their music, as by this point, most non-classical groups were using some electronic equipment in their music. This form of Electronica included artists like Björk, Goldfrapp and Moby.

3) Most Electronica groups use instruments like drum machines, synthesizers and sub bass. Sub bass is a bass line that's lower than a normal electric bass guitar. It makes the speakers shake when it's played loud enough — you can really feel the music.

4) Lots of Electronica music has breakbeats — syncopated rhythms or polyrhythms (see p. 64) used in electronic music.

5) Electronica groups often use influences from other types of music like folk and world music. This makes even more sub-genres of Electronica — e.g. Folktronica uses elements of Electronica and folk music.

There are No Rules of Composition

Electronica artists vary a lot in terms of the style of music, the electronic instruments they use, their typical audience and their performance style.

1) Live performances often use more than one laptop so that the artists can use different effects on different programs at the same time.

2) They're composing and sequencing live, so every performance is different.

3) They use techniques and ideas from 'Musique Concrète' (see p. 48). They can turn samples of almost anything into music.

4) Performers use as many effects (like looping or pitch shifting — see p. 49) as they want.

5) Sounds are manipulated in different ways, so they often can't be copied exactly by other artists.

6) Just about all the sounds of the instruments are altered in some way.

7) A lot of Electronica is polyphonic (different lines weaving in and out of each other).

Moby uses Other Influences

Some Electronica artists (like Moby) use ideas from lots of other types of music — his music has ambient, hip-hop and techno influences.

1) Ambient music is also known as 'chill-out music'. It's very slow and calm — it's often used in clubs to create a more relaxing atmosphere for the clubbers when they want a break from dancing.

2) Hip-hop music is the music of the hip-hop culture that appeared in the Bronx, New York in the 1970s. It has Jamaican and African-American influences (like the drumbeats) and includes a lot of rapping (or 'toasting').

3) Techno is a type of club dance music that has a very fast beat. It sounds very mechanical and electronic.

Stressed about exams — listen to some ambient music...

Beatboxing came from hip-hop music — it's where you make percussion noises using only your voice. It's not just used in hip-hop music — there are even beatboxing world championships for male and female beatboxers. Justin Timberlake uses beatboxing on some of his albums, and some rappers and DJs use it too.

Moby — Why Does My Heart Feel So Bad?

Your set piece is Moby's _Why Does My Heart Feel So Bad?_ from his album 'Play'. You need to make sure you're <u>familiar</u> with the bits of <u>electronic equipment</u> used in this type of music — if you're a bit shaky, have a look over the last few pages for a quick reminder.

Moby's real name is Richard Melville Hall

1) <u>Richard Melville Hall</u> was born in America in <u>1965</u>. <u>Moby</u> was a nickname his parents gave him.
2) When he was young, he learnt <u>guitar</u>, <u>piano</u> and <u>drums</u>.
3) His music covers a <u>wide range</u> of genres — from <u>punk</u> to <u>rock</u> to <u>Electronica</u>. He's also <u>remixed</u> music by artists like <u>The Prodigy</u> and <u>Michael Jackson</u>, and <u>written</u> songs for <u>Sophie Ellis-Bextor</u> and <u>Britney Spears</u>.
4) Lots of his music has been used in <u>films</u>, like <u>Tomorrow Never Dies</u> and <u>The Bourne Identity</u>.
5) Moby uses a lot of <u>samples</u> in his music (see p. 49).

'Play' was released in 1999

1) Moby's album 'Play' was released in <u>1999</u>. It stayed at <u>number 1</u> in the UK album charts for over a month in 2000.
2) It was his first real <u>mainstream</u> pop success — before 'Play', most of his music was only popular as <u>electronic dance music</u> (though lots of the tracks on 'Play' are <u>dance tracks</u> too).
3) All the songs on the album have been used in <u>films</u>, <u>TV programmes</u> and <u>adverts</u>.
4) He uses <u>samples</u> of <u>Gospel</u>, <u>folk</u> and <u>rock music</u>.
5) Some of the tracks on the album are completely <u>electronic</u>, while others have more of a <u>rock</u> influence.

Why Does My Heart Feel So Bad? is from 'Play'

1) The track _Why Does My Heart Feel So Bad?_ is the fourth track on the album 'Play'. It was released in <u>November 1999</u> and got to <u>number 16</u> in the UK charts.
2) It was used in the trailer for the film _Black Hawk Down_, and also in an <u>advert</u> for a brand of <u>Portuguese beer</u>.
3) Most of the piece is made up of <u>samples</u> — Moby uses samples of a <u>Gospel choir</u> and a <u>hip-hop drumbeat</u> (see p. 50). The drumbeat sample has been <u>adjusted</u> to fit to the <u>tempo</u> of the piece.
4) He also uses <u>synthesized strings</u>, a <u>sub bass</u> (see p. 50) and a <u>keyboard</u>.

The Vocal Samples haven't been Altered

1) Moby uses <u>two</u> different <u>vocal samples</u> from a recording of <u>The Shining Light Gospel Choir</u> taken in <u>1953</u>.
2) He didn't <u>change</u> the recordings — any <u>background noise</u> has been <u>left in</u>.
3) He uses the sample 'Why does my heart feel so bad? Why does my soul feel so bad?' as the <u>verse</u>, and 'These open doors' as a <u>chorus</u>. He also makes a <u>loop</u> of 'These open doors'.

This 8-bar vocal sample makes up the verse...

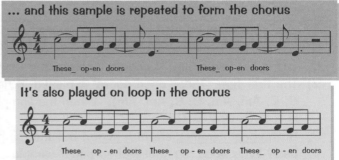

... and this sample is repeated to form the chorus

It's also played on loop in the chorus

My stomach feels bad — think it's indigestion...

Lots of the other tracks on 'Play' have been used in films and TV programmes — _Honey_ was used in the film _Holes_, _Porcelain_ was used in _The Beach_, _Bodyrock_ was used in _Ali_ and _Veronica's Closet_ was used in the TV series _Buffy the Vampire Slayer_. You'll probably recognize some of the tracks from these.

Moby — Why Does My Heart Feel So Bad?

The structure of this piece is quite straightforward, but make sure you can follow it and understand it in case it comes up in your exam.

The Texture builds up as Instruments are Added

1) Why Does My Heart Feel So Bad? is divided up into 8-bar sections (except for a 1-bar bridge about three-quarters of the way through the piece). It has a fairly standard pop structure (it goes intro, verse, chorus, verse, bridge, chorus, verse, outro).

2) The instrumentation's built up — more instruments are added in each section.

Bars	8	8	8	8	8	8	8	8	8	1	8	8	8	8
Piano introduction	■													
Piano rhythmic chords					■	■	■	■	■	■	■	■	■	
Voice 'Why does my heart...'		■	■	■				■						■
Voice 'Why does my heart...' (echo)								■						
Voice 'These open doors'					■									
Voice 'These open doors' (loop)						■					■	■		
Voice 'These open doors' (reverb)											■			
Sub bass			■	■	■	■	■	■	■		■	■	■	
Drums			■	■	■	■	■	■	■		■	■	■	
Synth strings melodic line			■	■	■	■	■	■	■					
Synth strings long notes				■	■	■	■	■	■		■	■	■	
Synth organ														■

The table gives you an idea of how it would look in a music program. The composer chooses a time frame and drags the sample he wants into the right position. Moby used Cubase.

The colours aren't just there to make it look pretty — they help the composer see where all the different tracks go.

3) It starts off with an 8-bar piano intro, then the verse starts. The 'Why does my heart feel so bad? Why does my soul feel so bad?' vocal sample's played 4 times. At first, there's just the piano playing in the background, then the hip-hop drumbeat, the sub bass and synthesized strings come in. The strings add melodic interest during the rests in the vocal line. On the third time through, more synthesized strings are added, playing long notes. The piano part then changes to rhythmic chords.

4) The chorus section uses the 'These open doors' vocal sample. It's played twice — once with rests in between the phrases, and once on loop. The backing in the chorus is both synth strings parts, the drumbeat, the sub bass and the rhythmic piano chords.

5) It goes back to the verse, using the same backing. The vocal sample is played twice, but with an echo part.

6) In the 1-bar bridge, the music seems to stop for a bar, but if you listen carefully, you can hear a pedal point (held on low note).

7) After the bridge, 'These open doors' is heard again — this time with a reverb effect. It's accompanied just by the long notes on the synthesized strings.

8) The 8-bar 'These open doors' loop is then played twice, over the rhythmic piano chords, sub bass, drums and long synth strings notes.

9) The piece finishes with one last 'Why does my heart feel so bad? Why does my soul feel so bad?', over the top of synthesized organ notes (the only time we hear the synth organ in the whole piece).

You need to know the Chords Moby uses

1) The 8-bar verse uses 4 chords, each lasting for two bars. These are A minor, E minor, G major and D major.

2) The first time 'These open doors' is played, it uses C major and A minor chords (the chord pattern goes C, C, Am, Am, C, C, Am, Am). When the sample's looped, an F major chord comes in — the chord pattern is F, F, C, C, F, F, C, C.

3) Both vocal samples are in A minor, but they're harmonised differently — the 'Why does my heart feel so bad? Why does my soul feel so bad?' sample sounds minor, as it's harmonised with mainly minor chords, but the 'These open doors' sample sounds major because of the chords used.

I wonder what a synthesized synthesizer sounds like...

Don't panic. I know this page looks a bit scary, but it's just describing the structure of the piece. Have another listen to it and try to follow the sections shown in the table and it'll all make sense.

Revision Summary

Aah, popular music... there's nothing like some phaser and breakbeats with a little light toasting to help you relax after a hard day revising GCSE Music. You'll probably be familiar with all kinds of popular music already but that doesn't mean you can listen to the radio for half an hour and call it revision. Ohhh no. You need to know the technical names for the different techniques and then be able to apply them to your set pieces in the exam to boot. Now, on to the revision summary of joy...

1)   Write down the seven notes of the Blues scale starting on C.
2)   Write down the chord pattern of the 12-bar blues (using I, II, III, IV etc).
3)   Describe the call and response pattern in the 12-bar blues.
4)   When and where did Jazz music develop?
5)   What is swing music?
6)   What are syncopated rhythms?
7)   When was 'Kind of Blue' by Miles Davis released?
8)   Give four ways that Miles Davis' solos changed the way jazz music was played.
9)   Is 'Kind of Blue' based on scales or chords?
10) What time signature is used in *All Blues*?
11) How does Davis create a mellow timbre in *All Blues*?
12) When and how does Davis change the traditional 12-bar blues chord pattern (it happens twice)?
13) Which six instruments make up the band which plays *All Blues*?
14) Four instruments take turns to play in the improvised section of *All Blues*. Which instruments are they and what order do they play in?
15) In 1990s rock music, which two notes are used in 'power chords'?
16) When did Jeff Buckley release the album 'Grace'?
17) What is the song *Grace* about?
18) What is falsetto?
19) What time signature is used in *Grace*? What time signature are rock songs usually in?
20) Describe the basic structure of *Grace*.
21) Name and explain two of the electronic effects used in *Grace*.
22) What key is used for the main section of *Grace*?
23) Explain the function of the following electronic equipment:
     a) synthesizer   b) sequencer   c) sampler.
24) What is sub bass?
25) What is meant by ambient music and where might you hear it played?
26) Give a definition of techno music.
27) When did Moby release *Why Does My Heart Feel So Bad*?
28) Give two types of music which Moby samples in *Why Does My Heart Feel So Bad?*.
29) Name three instruments which play in *Why Does My Heart Feel So Bad?*.
30) Describe the structure of *Why Does My Heart Feel So Bad?*.
31) Which sequencer program does Moby use in *Why Does My Heart Feel So Bad?*.
32) The 8-bar verse of *Why Does My Heart Feel So Bad?* features 4 chords which last for 2 bars each. What are the four chords?
33) Describe the two sets of chords used to accompany the 'These open doors' vocal sample in *Why Does My Heart Feel So Bad?*.
34) What key is used in the vocal samples?

British Folk Music

Even if you think you don't know anything about folk music you probably do. You've probably heard drunks singing <u>Auld Lang Syne</u> at New Year, or had to do <u>country dancing</u> at primary school — it's *that* kind of music.

Folk music was played by Ordinary People

1) Folk music's still around nowadays but it used to be <u>much more popular</u>. In olden times, before radios and record players, the <u>only</u> music ordinary people had was music they played themselves.

2) The tunes tend to be quite <u>simple</u> and work with just a <u>few</u> instruments or voices. This made them easier for Jo Bloggs in the pub, or field, or factory, to learn and play.

3) Folk music was hardly ever written down. It survived through the <u>oral tradition</u> — people heard a song or tune they liked and <u>memorised</u> it.

4) Folk music changes over time as people add <u>new ideas</u>. Sometimes they're being deliberately <u>creative</u>, sometimes they <u>can't remember</u> exactly what they've heard and make up a new bit to fill the gap.

5) The instruments used to play along with folk songs and dances tend to be <u>small</u> and <u>easy to carry</u>. The most popular ones are the <u>pipe and tabor</u> (a three-holed recorder and a drum, played together for a one-man band effect), the <u>fiddle</u>, the <u>hurdy-gurdy</u>, the <u>bagpipes</u>, the <u>accordion</u> and the <u>concertina</u>.

These are the main types of Folk Music...

WORKSONGS
- British worksongs were made up by people like <u>farm workers</u>, <u>builders</u>, <u>sailors</u> and <u>miners</u>.
- They sang to take their minds off the grind of <u>hard labour</u>, and to help them work as a <u>team</u>.
- The songs are <u>unaccompanied</u> — the workers didn't have spare hands for playing instruments.
- Lots of songs were in <u>call and response</u> style. The '<u>shantyman</u>' sang the story and the other men joined in the <u>chorus</u>.

BALLADS
- Ballads tell <u>stories</u>.
- Some stories are made up — they tell stories from legends or about love affairs.
- Other ballads are about real events like shipwrecks or battles. Before <u>radios</u> and <u>television</u> when many people <u>couldn't read</u>, ballads were a way of passing on the news.

SHORT SONGS
- There are tons of shorter songs with <u>romantic</u> or <u>comic</u> lyrics.

DANCE MUSIC
- At events like <u>weddings</u> and <u>parties</u> people danced to <u>live music</u>.
- Lots of these dances are still around today — you still see people doing <u>Morris dances</u>, <u>sword dances</u>, <u>Scottish Highland dancing</u> and <u>Irish dancing</u>.

Folk tunes are fairly Simple

Some use <u>modal scales</u>.

T'ain't <u>simple</u>. I'm usin' two 'ands.

1) A lot of folk <u>melodies</u> are based on <u>pentatonic</u> scales. They've only got <u>five notes</u>, which makes writing tunes with them lots easier.

2) A <u>major pentatonic</u> scale uses notes <u>1</u>, <u>2</u>, <u>3</u>, <u>5</u> and <u>6</u> of an ordinary <u>major scale</u>.

3) A <u>minor pentatonic</u> scale uses notes <u>1</u>, <u>3</u>, <u>4</u>, <u>5</u> and <u>7</u> of a <u>natural minor scale</u>.

4) There are <u>no semitone intervals</u> in pentatonic scales. It makes it much easier to add a <u>harmony</u> because the notes don't clash. It also makes them <u>easy to sing</u>.

The <u>structure</u> in folk tunes tends to be pretty simple too. <u>Songs</u> are often <u>strophic</u> — the tune stays the same for each verse. Strophic songs can either be a number of <u>musically identical</u> verses (with different words), or can have a <u>chorus</u> that's just a <u>slight variation</u> on the verse (so the structure's AA'AA'A...). Phrases have even numbers of bars — usually <u>four</u>. Often each phrase begins with an <u>anacrusis</u> (upbeat).

And dosey-do...

Folk music is played by <u>ordinary people</u> — it's more beer and wellies than champagne and black tie. The main thing to remember is that the pentatonic scale makes writing melody and harmony <u>way easier</u>.

Capercaillie — Skye Waulking Song

Every <u>country</u> in the world has its own type of <u>folk music</u>. The music uses <u>local languages</u>, <u>dialects</u> and <u>instruments</u>, so it's <u>different</u> in different places — sometimes even from <u>village</u> to <u>village</u>.

Lots of Celtic Folk Music comes from Scotland and Ireland

1) Lots of places in <u>Western Europe</u> have traditional Celtic folk music — like <u>Wales</u>, <u>Cornwall</u> and <u>Brittany</u> in France.
2) Celtic folk music also includes <u>traditional Scottish</u> and <u>Irish</u> music.
3) The songs are often sung in <u>Gaelic</u>, traditional Celtic languages spoken in Scotland and Ireland. The two most common forms are <u>Scots Gaelic</u> and <u>Irish Gaelic</u> — some people in Scotland and Ireland <u>still</u> speak Scots and Irish Gaelic.
4) Traditional Celtic instruments include <u>fiddles</u>, <u>bagpipes</u>, <u>tin whistles</u> and <u>accordions</u>. An Irish framed drum called the <u>bodhrán</u> is also used.
5) Some bands turn folk music into a more <u>modern</u> style by adding a <u>bass</u> line and <u>drum kit</u> — bands like <u>Capercaillie</u> and <u>Runrig</u> have made Celtic folk music really popular.

Capercaillie is a Celtic Folk Band

1) Capercaillie is a <u>modern folk band</u>. It's made up of <u>eight</u> musicians mainly from <u>Scotland</u> and <u>Ireland</u> (though one's from <u>Manchester</u>). It was formed in <u>Oban</u> in Scotland in <u>1984</u>, and has become famous <u>worldwide</u>.
2) They play <u>traditional</u> folk instruments — <u>Uilleann pipes</u>, <u>flute</u>, <u>fiddle</u>, <u>accordion</u> and <u>bouzouki</u> (a string instrument a bit like a <u>mandolin</u>) over the top of more <u>modern</u> instruments like <u>drums</u>, <u>piano/keyboard</u> and <u>bass guitar</u>.
3) Their <u>singer</u>'s called <u>Karen Matheson</u> — she mainly sings in <u>Scots Gaelic</u>.
4) Their music is a <u>mix</u> of <u>traditional Celtic</u> songs and more <u>contemporary</u> ideas — they blend <u>traditional instruments</u> and <u>ideas</u> with <u>modern drumbeats</u>.
5) They've sold over <u>1 million</u> albums and are popular all over the world. They also appeared in and wrote some music for the film *Rob Roy*.

Waulking is a part of Clothmaking

1) '<u>Waulking</u>' is a name for a stage in traditional <u>clothmaking</u> — woollen cloth or tweed was <u>cleaned</u>, <u>thickened</u> and <u>softened</u> by this process. Women <u>pounded</u> the cloth against a table or <u>trampled</u> on it.
2) The women would <u>sing songs</u> to <u>pass the time</u> and <u>keep the rhythm</u> of the pounding. They needed to move the cloth <u>in time</u> with each other, and singing helped them do this — the songs have a strong <u>rhythm</u>. It also <u>lifted their spirits</u> — waulking was hard work.
3) Songs could last for well over an hour. One woman would sing the <u>verses</u>, and the rest would join in on the <u>choruses</u>.

Skye Waulking Song is from the album 'Nàdurra'

1) Capercaillie released their album '<u>Nàdurra</u>' in <u>2000</u>. 'Nàdurra' is Gaelic for '<u>naturally</u>'.
2) The full title of the piece is *Chuir M'Athair Mise Dhan Taigh Charraideach (Skye Waulking Song)*, which translates as '<u>My Father Sent Me to a House of Sorrow</u>'.

Skye's the limit...

The band was named after the capercaillie (or wood grouse), a large bird. It's found all over Northern Europe, but in the British Isles it's only found in Scotland. Capercaillies are under threat though — there are less than 2,000 left in Scotland and they're at risk of extinction. Save the capercaillie.

Capercaillie — Skye Waulking Song

Skye Waulking Song brings together traditional folk music with elements of pop music.

The song is in Two Sections

1) Skye Waulking Song is divided into two main sections.
2) The melody is based on a pentatonic scale (see p. 54).
3) It's in 6/8, with two beats in a bar. The strong rhythm helped the workers keep in time.
4) It's played on a mix of traditional and modern instruments. The fiddle, pipes, whistle, accordion and bouzouki are all traditional, while the guitar, bass guitar, drum kit and keyboard are more modern. They all play in their middle range — there are no high-pitched screeching notes.
5) It has a polyrhythmic texture — lots of different rhythms are being played at the same time. The singer's part has a different rhythm to the rest of the band. At some points, the singer's part is in 6/8, while the hi-hat's playing 3 crotchets in a bar, making it feel like 3/4.
6) It has a fade-out ending.

Some of the features are different in the two different sections:

SECTION ONE
- The first section feels very traditional, with just a simple beat.
- It's in E minor — the chords change between Em and G.
- It's quite quiet, calm and peaceful — it sounds almost subdued.
- None of the instruments really stand out in this section — the focus is on the singer.

SECTION TWO
- The full rhythm section (drums and bass part) play in the second section and drive it forward.
- It's in G major (the relative major of E minor).
- It's generally much louder, though there's a quieter bit when the drums and bass guitar stop.
- There's a pipe solo that uses some of the vocal melody line in its improvisation. There are harmonised backing vocals too.

The Lyrics are in Scots Gaelic

1) The lyrics to Skye Waulking Song are in Scots Gaelic. It has two main verses and two 'inserts' (called 'seisd 1' and 'seisd 2'). 'Seisd' is pronounced 'shesht'. Seisd 1 is 'Hi ri huraibhi o ho' and seisd 2 is 'O hi a bho ro hu o ho'. After each line of the verse, one of the inserts is sung (though the introductory vocal part starts with seisd 1) — so the first part of verse 1 (after a few introductory lines) goes:

> Chuir m'athair mise dha'n taigh charraideach
> Hi ri huraibhi o ho   ← SEISD 1
> 'N oidhche sin a rinn e bhanais dhomh
> O hi a bho ro hu o ho   ← SEISD 2

The inserts are an example of vocables — nonsense syllables like 'Hey nonny nonny' and 'Fa la la'. Vocables are an important part of traditional folk music — these are the lines that everyone can join in.

2) The lines of the verses are taken directly from a 13th century lament called Seathan, Mac Righ Eireann ('Seathan, Son of the King of Ireland'). It's about a girl who's unhappy with the marriage her father's arranged for her.
3) The two verses are divided up by the pipe solo.
4) The structure's a bit different to traditional waulking songs — they would have a verse-chorus structure, where one woman would sing the verses and the rest would join in with the choruses. As Skye Waulking Song is a modern version of a waulking song, Capercaillie didn't stick to the traditional form — they have the two verses and two inserts but no chorus. Skye Waulking Song has a strophic structure — the melody is the same for both verses.

It's all Gaelic to me...

You need to make sure you know the key features of this piece, and which bits are typical of folk music. Make sure you know about waulking too — that'll really impress the examiners (it'll help if you can explain why they sang while they were working — that bit's covered on the previous page). Hey nonny nonny.

Indian Raga

This is the section where you look at music from other parts of the world. The music's great, but you need to make sure you can <u>spell all the words</u> if you want to write about them in the exam.

Indian Classical Music is based on Ragas

1) A <u>raga</u> is a <u>set of notes</u> (usually between 5 and 8) which are combined to create a particular <u>mood</u>.

2) Raga performances are <u>improvised</u>, but based on traditional tunes and rhythms. These are <u>never written down</u> — they're passed on from generation to generation <u>aurally</u>.

3) Ragas use a scale similar to the Western 12-note scale. But while the Western scale is <u>tempered</u> (there's the same distance between neighbouring notes), the raga scale is not — the intervals can vary.

4) In Northern India, raga students join a school of players called a <u>gharana</u>. Each gharana is run by a teacher or 'master' and each gharana has its own traditions and theories about how to play.

5) <u>Spirituality</u> is an important part of almost all Indian Classical Music. In Southern India, there is a long tradition of the <u>Karnatic kriti</u>. This is a raga set to words in praise of a particular <u>Hindu deity</u>.

The Sitar, Tambura and Tabla are Traditional Instruments

SITAR

1) A <u>sitar</u> is a large, long-necked <u>string</u> instrument.

2) On a seven-stringed sitar, five of the strings are plucked for the <u>melody</u> and the other two create <u>drone</u> notes.

3) Sitars also have '<u>sympathetic</u>' strings <u>underneath</u> the main strings. The sympathetic strings <u>vibrate</u> when the main strings are played, creating a thick, shimmery sound.

4) The <u>frets</u> on a sitar can be moved — they're <u>adjusted</u> to different positions for different pieces.

5) Sitar players can pull strings to make notes '<u>bend</u>' or distort.

6) Sliding a finger along a string as it's plucked gives a sliding glissando sound called <u>mind</u>.

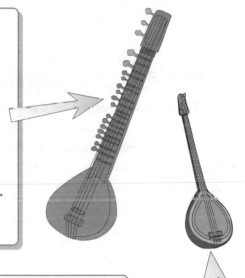

TAMBURA (also called TANPURA)

The tambura's a similar shape to the sitar. It usually has <u>four</u> metal strings, but can have up to <u>six</u>. It's used as more of a <u>backing</u> instrument.

TABLA

Tabla is a <u>pair</u> of drums. The smaller, right-hand drum is called the <u>tabla</u> (also called the <u>dayan</u>). The larger, lower-sounding drum is called the <u>bayan</u>.

OTHER INSTRUMENTS ARE USED TOO...

1) The <u>sarod</u> — an instrument like a small <u>sitar</u> with a <u>fretless</u> fingerboard.

2) The <u>sarangi</u> — a small, <u>bowed</u> stringed instrument with <u>no frets</u>.

3) The <u>bansuri</u> (or <u>venu</u>) — a <u>flute</u> made of <u>bamboo</u>.

4) The <u>shehnai</u> — an instrument with a <u>double reed</u>, like an oboe.

5) The <u>harmonium</u> — a <u>keyboard instrument</u> powered with air pumped by hand bellows.

6) <u>Singers</u> sometimes perform with the instruments as well.

Indian Raga

Each instrument in raga has a different job. The <u>sitar</u> often plays the <u>melody</u>. The <u>tabla</u> play the <u>rhythm</u>. You'll have to wait till the next page to find out about the tambura. (Can you bear the <u>suspense</u>...)

The Melody is Improvised on the Sitar

1) In a classical Indian group the sitar often plays the <u>melody</u>.

2) The sitar player <u>improvises</u> the melody. He or she chooses a <u>raga</u> (see p. 57), and makes up the melody using notes from it.

3) There are <u>hundreds</u> of different ragas. Each one is named after a different <u>time of day</u> or <u>season</u>. Each raga's supposed to create an <u>atmosphere</u> like the time or season it's named after.

4) Each raga is a set of <u>ascending</u> and <u>descending</u> notes. The notes on the way up can be different from the ones on the way down.

5) Some ragas have rules for individual notes. There could be notes that are always played <u>quickly</u>, notes that have to be <u>decorated</u>, or notes have to be played <u>tivra</u> (slightly sharp) or <u>komal</u> (slightly flat).

6) The notes of a raga are called <u>sa</u>, <u>ri</u>, <u>ga</u>, <u>ma</u>, <u>pa</u>, <u>dha</u> and <u>ni</u>. Unlike Western scales, ragas don't always have the full set of notes.

7) Sometimes the melody part's taken by a <u>singer</u> instead of the sitar.

RAGA VIBHASA — DAWN RAGA

SA   RI   GA   MA DHA SA DHA   MA   GA   RI   SA

The Tabla is the Rhythm section

1) The main rhythm is played on the <u>tabla</u>.

2) The tabla player plays a rhythm called a <u>tala</u> with a set number of beats (called <u>matras</u>). There are hundreds of talas, just like there are hundreds of ragas.

3) The <u>first beat</u> of a tala is called the <u>sam</u>. <u>All</u> the performers in a group <u>play together</u> on each sam and the whole piece always <u>ends</u> on a sam.

4) Each tala is split into groups called <u>vibhags</u>. A vibhag is a bit like a <u>bar</u> in Western music, except that you can have different numbers of beats in each vibhag.

5) One, or sometimes two, vibhags in a tala have a <u>different sound</u> from the others — this section's called the <u>vibhag khali</u>. For contrast, the vibhag khali is played on the <u>smaller</u> tabla drum.

6) As well as playing the tala, tabla players improvise <u>more complicated rhythms</u> over the top. They can vary their sound with different <u>finger positions</u>, and by <u>speaking</u> the beat (with syllables like <u>dhin</u> or <u>ta</u>) as they play.

7) Sometimes the <u>audience</u> joins in, and claps along with the tala. They clap at the beginning of each vibhag. In the vibhag khali they do a quiet clap, called a <u>wave</u>, tapping the back of the right hand into the left.

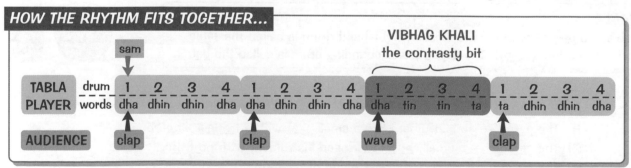

HOW THE RHYTHM FITS TOGETHER...

		sam								VIBHAG KHALI the contrasty bit						
TABLA	drum	1	2	3	4	1	2	3	4	1	2	3	4	1	2	3	4
PLAYER	words	dha	dhin	dhin	dha	dha	dhin	dhin	dha	dha	tin	tin	ta	ta	dhin	dhin	dha
AUDIENCE		clap				clap				wave				clap			

Can we have a tabla for four, please...

Some people find it tricky to get to grips with raga because it's so different from the music they're used to. That's <u>precisely why</u> the examiners make you study it — you're supposed to be amazed at the great and glorious diversity of music. You're probably meant to be grateful too. <u>How</u> grateful you feel is up to you.

Indian Raga

To complete the sound of raga you add the <u>tambura</u> to the sitar and tabla.

The Tambura creates the Harmony

1) The <u>tambura</u>'s job in a raga performance is to create the <u>harmony</u>. The sitar part is a bit like the right-hand part in a piano piece and the tambura's like the left.

2) The tambura's part is often described as a <u>drone</u>. It's not quite as boring as the name suggests, but it is quite <u>repetitive</u>. The tambura player plays a <u>simple rhythmic pattern</u> based on just <u>two notes</u> from the raga all the way through the performance.

3) The sitar player works his or her improvisations <u>around</u> the tambura part — and it's the combination of the two that gives the raga harmony.

> *Usually the drone uses the '<u>sa</u>' and '<u>pa</u>' notes, but the one for the Raga Vibhasa uses '<u>sa</u>' and '<u>dha</u>'.*

SA DHA DHA SA

I'll do the droning round here if you don't mind.

A typical raga has Four Sections

The tradition is for a raga performance to have <u>four phases</u>.
There are <u>no gaps</u> between the different phases — each one flows into the next.

1 THE ALAP

The <u>sitar</u> player introduces the notes of the chosen <u>raga</u>, improvising freely. There's <u>no beat</u> or pulse to the melody at this point — it just flows along. The only accompaniment at this point is the <u>tambura drone</u>.

2 THE JHOR

In this second section, the music <u>speeds up</u> a bit. It's still just the tambura player and sitar player, but the music gets more rhythmic, and the melody improvised by the sitar player takes on a <u>steady beat</u>.

3 THE JHALA

This section is <u>loads faster</u> than the alap and jhor, and feels a lot more exciting than the bits that came before. The players improvise around the melody.

4 THE GAT OR BANDISH

In the gat, the raga really takes off.

- The <u>tabla player</u> comes in — at last.
- The group plays a <u>pre-composed</u> piece. It's called a 'gat' if it's for instruments only, and a 'bandish' if there's a song.
- The players also add improvisations to the gat or bandish, and pass their musical ideas around in a sort of musical <u>question and answer</u>.

I hope you're gatting this...

I reckon the trickiest bit here isn't <u>understanding</u> it — it's remembering the massive number of words that are completely new unless you've studied raga before. But they're just words — like <u>egg</u> and <u>car park</u>. Close the book and scribble down all those technical words and what they mean. And keep at it.

Rag Desh

This part of the specification is a bit different to the others — you have <u>three</u> pieces to listen to instead of just one, and they're just <u>suggested</u> pieces to listen to — you <u>might</u> get a <u>different version</u> in your exam. They're all based on the same <u>raga</u> (see p. 57) — the <u>Rag Desh</u>.

Rag Desh is the Rainy Season Raga

1) Each raga is meant to be played at a <u>specific time of day</u> during a <u>specific season</u>. They're supposed to <u>create certain moods</u>. The <u>Rag Desh</u> is supposed to be played at <u>night</u> during the <u>rainy season</u>. It's meant to give the feeling of <u>romance</u> and <u>devotion</u>.

2) You have to look at <u>three</u> different versions of Rag Desh — one from the album '<u>Priyagitah: The Nightingale</u>' (performed by <u>Steve Gorn</u> and <u>Benjy Wertheimer</u>), another from '<u>Live at Carnegie Hall</u>' by <u>Anoushka Shankar</u> and the third from the album '<u>Mewar Re Mira</u>' by <u>S. D. Dhandhada</u> and <u>H. Dhandhada</u>. Instead of the third raga, your teacher might have a similar version by <u>Chiranji Lal Tanwar</u>. They're both OK with Edexcel.

3) Even though they all sound very different, they're all based on this <u>raga</u>:

SA RI MA PA NI SA <u>NI</u> DHA PA MA GA RI SA

N.B. The ascending pattern is <u>different</u> to the descending one — there are <u>more notes</u> on the way down and <u>ni</u> is <u>flattened</u>.

'Priyagitah' was recorded in a Studio

1) Steve Gorn and Benjy Wertheimer's version of Rag Desh was <u>improvised</u> in a <u>recording studio</u>. It's based around the <u>traditional raga structure</u> (see p. 59), but there are a few <u>differences</u> — some <u>modern</u> ragas <u>miss out</u> some sections to keep the audience's <u>attention</u>.

2) This version is divided up into <u>three</u> tracks on the CD — the first is the <u>alap</u>, then the second two are both <u>gats</u>. Each gat's based on a different <u>tala</u> (see p. 58).

3) At the beginning of the <u>alap</u>, you can hear the <u>tambura drone</u>. Then the <u>bansuri</u> and <u>esraj</u> (an instrument that's quite like a <u>sarangi</u> but with frets) come in. They <u>improvise</u> using the notes of the Rag Desh. This section is quite <u>slow</u> and <u>flowing</u> — there's <u>no pulse</u> to drive it along.

The melodic instruments in this Rag Desh are the <u>bansuri</u> (a bamboo flute) and the <u>esraj</u> (a bowed string instrument with frets). Make sure you can identify them.

4) In the next section, the <u>tabla</u> comes in, playing a <u>steady rhythm</u>. The bansuri plays another improvised melody. It's a bit <u>faster</u> than the alap. This gat is based on the <u>rupak</u> tala, which has <u>7 beats</u>.

5) In the final track (the second gat), the raga is a lot <u>faster</u>. The <u>tabla</u> plays a <u>fast complicated rhythm</u> using the <u>12-beat ektal</u> tala. The bansuri plays over the top of it, but the melody is much more <u>structured</u>. It's now playing a <u>pre-composed</u> melody with lots of <u>runs</u>. It's still based on the Rag Desh.

The rainy season in the UK — that'll be April to March...

There's a chance you'll be asked what <u>notes</u> are in the Rag Desh, so make sure you <u>learn</u> what they are. Remember that the notes on the way down are <u>different</u> to the ones on the way up. Practise writing the raga out from <u>memory</u>. It'd be useful to know <u>when</u> the Rag Desh is meant to be played as well.

Rag Desh

The three versions of Rag Desh all sound very <u>different</u> — even though they're based on the <u>same raga</u>.
This is true of <u>all</u> Indian music — no two performances of a raga are the same.
The <u>improvised</u> nature of the music means there can be lots of different <u>interpretations</u> of it.

Anoushka Shankar plays the Sitar

1) <u>Anoushka Shankar</u> is a classically-trained <u>pianist</u>, <u>conductor</u> and <u>sitar player</u>. She's the daughter of <u>Ravi Shankar</u>, an Indian musician who's famous all over the world. He taught her to play the sitar.

2) This version of Rag Desh was recorded <u>live</u> at the <u>Carnegie Hall</u> in New York. It was composed by Ravi Shankar, and Anoushka's accompanied by two <u>tabla</u> players — <u>Bikram Ghosh</u> and <u>Tanmoy Bose</u>. There's also a <u>tambura drone</u>.

3) It's made up of an <u>alap</u> and two different <u>gats</u>.

4) In the alap, when there's just the <u>sitar</u> and <u>tambura</u> playing, you can hear the different <u>techniques</u> Anoushka Shankar uses — she <u>strums</u>, <u>plucks</u> and <u>bends</u> notes. Bent notes are made by <u>pulling</u> the string to <u>change</u> the sound.

5) The first gat uses a <u>10-beat</u> tala called the <u>jhaptal</u>. The second gat is a bit <u>faster</u> and uses the 16-beat <u>tintal</u> tala. In both, Anoushka Shankar is playing a <u>pre-composed melody</u>.

6) This rag desh is all on <u>one track</u> — there are no <u>gaps</u> between the different sections. You have to listen out for the changes in <u>tempo</u> and the <u>tabla</u> coming in.

'Mewar Re Mira' has a Singer

1) The version of Rag Desh on the album '<u>Mewar Re Mira</u>' uses a <u>voice</u> to sing the raga. It's performed by <u>S. D. Dhandhada</u> and <u>H. Dhandhada</u>. It was recorded in a <u>studio</u>. The <u>Chiranji Lal Tanwar</u> version also has a <u>male singer</u>.

2) In the <u>alap</u>, the <u>sitar</u> improvises using the notes of the <u>raga</u> over a <u>tambura drone</u>. It's joined by a <u>sarangi</u>, then the <u>voice</u> comes in. The singer is <u>male</u>, and uses a lot of <u>vibrato</u>. He also <u>scoops</u> notes — starts on a different note then <u>slides</u> to the right one (also called a <u>portamento</u>). It's quite a <u>short</u> alap.

3) The <u>tempo</u> increases in the next section, and the <u>tabla</u> comes in.

4) In the final section (the <u>bandish</u> — like a gat but with a singer), the vocal part becomes more <u>elaborate</u>. There are lots of <u>trills</u> and <u>portamentos</u>. <u>Hand cymbals</u> are also used towards the end.

> This might be <u>slightly different</u> to the piece your teacher has shown you — but <u>don't worry</u>, you can still use these points in the exam.

You need to Identify the Instruments

1) It's <u>important</u> that you can <u>spot</u> which <u>instruments</u> are being played in the different versions of the Rag Desh. Each one has a different instrument playing the <u>main melody</u> — the <u>bansuri</u> in 'Priyagitah: The Nightingale', the <u>sitar</u> in 'Live at Carnegie Hall' and a <u>male singer</u> in 'Mewar Re Mira'.

2) You'll also need to be able to <u>identify</u> the different <u>sections</u> of the music — see p. 59 for a detailed description of each bit.

3) Make sure you can describe the <u>differences</u> between the extracts too — mention the <u>instruments</u>, the <u>tempos</u> and even whether the melody is <u>improvised</u> or <u>pre-composed</u>.

Large, sympathetic sitar seeks childcare opportunities...

Phew. I bet you're glad that section's over — there's lots of <u>tricky names</u> to learn. Make sure you know them <u>all</u> — you'll be throwing away <u>easy marks</u> if you haven't learnt the names of the <u>different sections</u> of a raga, or don't know which <u>instruments</u> are used. Once you know them, you're well on your way.

African Music

This section's called 'African Music', but you don't have to learn about every type of African music. The music you need to learn about is from <u>sub-Saharan Africa</u>. That means the massive area <u>south of the Sahara</u>.

Drums play a big part in African Culture

1) Drums are probably the <u>most widely played instrument</u> in Africa.
2) In tribal society, drums get a lot of <u>respect</u> — they're thought of as one of the best instruments.
3) Drums are used to play an <u>accompaniment</u> for <u>singing</u>, <u>dancing</u> and even <u>working</u>.
4) Drums are also used to <u>call people together</u> for important <u>community events</u> like weddings and funerals — a bit like church bells in Europe. There are <u>different drum beats</u> for different events, so people from <u>neighbouring villages</u> can tell what's going on just by listening to the drums.
5) Most African drum music is passed on through <u>oral tradition</u> — it's not written down.

These are the Main Types of Drum...

1) The <u>djembe</u> is played in Guinea and Mali in West Africa. It has a <u>single head</u> and is shaped a bit like a <u>goblet</u>. It's played with the <u>hands</u>. The overall <u>size</u> of the drum affects its <u>pitch</u> — <u>smaller</u> drums are <u>higher-pitched</u>.

* not to scale

2) The <u>dundun</u> is played in Guinea and Mali too. Dundun are <u>cylindrical drums</u> played with <u>sticks</u>. There's a drum skin at each end, so they're played <u>horizontally</u>.

   There are three types:
   KENKENI — a high-pitched drum that keeps the pulse going,
   SANGBAN — a mid-pitched drum,
   DOUNDOUN — a large, low-pitched drum.

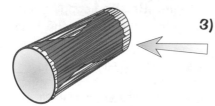

3) The <u>donno</u> from Ghana is also known as the <u>hourglass</u> or <u>talking</u> drum. The player holds it under one arm, and with the other arm hits the drumhead with a thin curved stick.

   The <u>vertical strings</u> round the sides attach to the drumhead. The player can <u>squeeze</u> and <u>release</u> the strings as they play to change the pitch of the drum.

4) The <u>kagan</u> (a small barrel-shaped drum) and the <u>kidi</u> (a medium-sized barrel drum) are both from Ghana.

The drums have lots of Different Names

1) Not only do the materials and playing styles vary from area to area — the <u>names</u> for similar designs of drums vary too.
2) The piece you have to study comes from <u>Burkina Faso</u>, a country in western Africa.
3) Burkina Faso's bordered by six countries, including <u>Mali</u> and <u>Ghana</u>. It's also quite close to <u>Guinea</u> as well — so the drums played in Burkina Faso have <u>similar</u> names to the ones played in these countries.

My drums are called Nigel and Dave...

Unless you've got a photographic memory, or are otherwise brilliantly gifted with powers of learning far beyond those of us ordinary mortals, you can't just go <u>skipping over</u> the names of the drums. Learn them. Learn how to spell them. Learn the facts about them. Learn it all now.

African Music

There are more African drums than you can shake a <u>stick</u> at (unless it's a drumstick of course).
You don't just need to learn the names — read on and find out <u>how you play 'em</u>.

Talking Drums are used to Send Messages

Skilled drummers can make drums '<u>talk</u>'. They <u>change the pitch</u> to
imitate changing pitch levels in ordinary <u>speech</u>. The drum sounds carry
over long distances, so they can be used to <u>send messages</u>.

There are literally <u>thousands</u> of different languages and dialects in Africa. Each drummer imitates his
own language to send messages. Drummers like to play on instruments made with <u>local materials</u>.
They believe that this <u>helps</u> the instrument 'speak' the local language.

What with local languages and materials for making drums being so varied, you get very
<u>different instruments</u> and <u>different playing styles</u> from area to area.

There's a big variety of Playing Techniques

There's a bit more to African drumming than hitting a drum with a stick or a
brush — there are several different <u>playing techniques</u>.

1) There are no prizes for guessing that one technique is hitting the drum with a <u>stick</u>.

2) A lot of African drummers also play using their <u>hands</u>. There are three basic strokes:

   * <u>slap</u> — hit the edge of the drum with the fingers splayed open
   * <u>tone</u> — hit the edge of the drum with the fingers held together
   * <u>bass</u> — hit the centre of the main drum skin with a flat hand.

3) <u>Dampening</u> is <u>resting</u> one <u>hand</u> or <u>stick</u> on the drum skin whilst playing with the other.

4) On some styles of drum you can <u>change pitch</u> as you're playing, by tightening the skin.

5) To get a <u>contrasting</u> sound you can <u>strike the wood</u> instead of the skin.

The Master Drummer leads the group

1) In most African drum ensembles there is a <u>master drummer</u>.
   He's accompanied by any number of other drums and percussion.

2) A system of <u>call</u> and <u>response</u> is used to <u>structure</u> the music:

   *The master drummer plays a <u>rhythmic signal</u> which sets the <u>tempo</u> and <u>rhythm</u> for the other
   players. After this call the other players join in with the response.
   This call and response pattern is usually repeated <u>many times</u> during a performance.*

3) The master drummer also <u>controls</u> the build-up and release of <u>tension</u>. He leads the other
   players in changes of <u>dynamics</u>, <u>tempo</u>, <u>pitch</u> and <u>rhythm</u>. In general the drum beats are
   quite repetitive — these changes are what keep the audience hooked.

*Call and response
is used in singing
too, especially for
church music.*

Dum-da-dum-da means "Come inside, it's teatime"...

Get those techniques off pat. (No, not off Pat. Pat knows nothing about drumming techniques.)
Get them off pat, learn them inside out and commit every detail to memory — when it comes to the
test they want <u>detailed</u> answers. "The drummers hit the drums" is nowhere near enough information.

African Music

Drums have a special place in African music but the <u>voice</u> and <u>other instruments</u> are important too.

The Thumb Piano, Balafon and Kora are popular

These are some of the most popular instruments apart from drums.

- A <u>BALAFON</u> (or <u>BALOPHONE</u>) is a wooden xylophone.
- It makes a <u>warm</u>, <u>mellow</u> sound.
- The lumpy things hanging under the keys are dried <u>gourds</u> (vegetables like pumpkins).
- It's mostly played in <u>West Africa</u>.

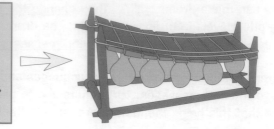

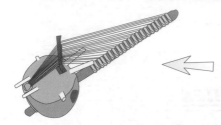

- The <u>KORA</u> is made and played by the Mandingo people.
- It's got <u>21 strings</u> and you play it by <u>plucking</u> — a bit like a harp.
- It's also mostly played in <u>West Africa</u>.

- The <u>MBIRA</u> or <u>THUMB PIANO</u> is really popular — partly because it's pocket-sized.
- It makes a <u>liquid</u>, <u>twangy</u> sound.
- It's played all over Africa.

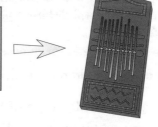

The Rhythms are Complex

1) African music is based on <u>rhythmic cycles</u> of varying lengths.
2) Drummers <u>accent</u> particular beats in a rhythmic cycle.
3) Sometimes different rhythmic cycles, with the accents in different places, are played <u>together</u> — this effect is called <u>polyrhythm</u>.
4) Sometimes you'll get <u>two</u> or <u>more</u> rhythms that don't fit easily together. They kind of fight against one another, creating <u>tension</u> in the music. The posh technical term for this effect is <u>cross-rhythm</u>.
5) You get a <u>syncopated</u> effect when you emphasise notes that don't fall on a strong beat.
6) Even though the music is based on repeated cycles, individual players introduce <u>small variations</u>. These gradually <u>develop</u> the basic patterns throughout the performance.

Performances are Long and Involve the Audience

Performances can last for several hours and involve an audience response — <u>shouting</u> and <u>cheering</u> or <u>repeating a phrase</u> sung by the main performers is an integral part of the performance. It's often <u>a capella</u> (unaccompanied singing).

African music often uses <u>call and response</u>. <u>Call and response</u> is a <u>spontaneous</u>, often <u>improvised</u> style of music where someone sings or plays a musical '<u>question</u>' and another <u>responds</u>.

Listen out for <u>call and response</u> in *Ladysmith Black Mambazo*'s work. They became world-famous when they featured on *Paul Simon's* album *Graceland*.

Polyrhythms — learn them parrot fashion...

This might not sound very exciting on paper. I think you've really got to hear a <u>recording</u> to "get it". Even then it's a bit hard to get into because you've got to hear the drums for quite a long time before you start to notice the changes. Then again, maybe you'll love it first time round — who am I to say?

Koko — Yiri

There's <u>more</u> to African music than just <u>drumming</u>. You need to know about <u>singing</u> too.

Singing is important in Sub-Saharan African Music

1) <u>Singing</u> is an essential part of <u>everyday life</u> in sub-Saharan Africa. Like traditional <u>folk music</u> from England, Ireland, Scotland and Wales, it's sung by <u>ordinary people</u>. It plays an important part in the <u>community</u>.

2) It's also a big part of <u>celebrations</u> and events like <u>birthdays</u>, <u>weddings</u>, <u>funerals</u>, <u>harvests</u> and <u>rituals</u>.

3) As well as singing, instruments like the <u>balafon</u>, <u>kora</u> and <u>mbira</u> are used to play <u>tunes</u> and create <u>harmony</u>. There's more about these instruments on p. 64.

4) Music is <u>passed down</u> from generation to generation, and <u>isn't</u> usually <u>written down</u>.

5) <u>Key features</u> of this type of music are:

> - <u>Cross-rhythms</u> and <u>polyrhythms</u> (see p. 64)
> - <u>Polyphony</u> (lots of parts weaving in and out of each other)
> - <u>Repetition</u>
> - <u>Call and response</u> (see p. 63-64)
> - <u>Heterophony</u> (all parts play different versions of the same tune at the same time, often at different pitches)
> - <u>Improvised melodies</u> (can sound a bit like theme and variation form — see p. 10)

Koko are from Burkina Faso

1) The group <u>Koko</u> come from <u>Burkina Faso</u> in Western Africa.

2) It's led by <u>Madou Koné</u>, who <u>sings</u> and plays the <u>balafon</u>. He was born in <u>Bobo Dioulasso</u>, a city in Burkina Faso that's famous for its music.

3) There are <u>five</u> other members of the group. They play other percussion instruments like the <u>dundun</u>, the <u>djembe</u> and the <u>donno</u> (see p. 62). Some of them also <u>sing</u>.

4) The <u>themes</u> of their songs are:
   - The <u>struggle to survive</u> in day-to-day life.
   - The importance of the <u>environment</u> and how it should be <u>protected</u>.
   - <u>Creation</u> and the <u>celebration of life</u>.
   - The importance of <u>friendship</u>.
   - The importance of their <u>surroundings</u> and the <u>earth</u>.

5) Koko's music is <u>typical</u> of Burkina Faso — it includes a lot of <u>drumming</u> and <u>balafon playing</u>, as well as <u>singing</u>.

6) The track <u>Yiri</u> comes from their album '<u>Burkina Faso — Balafons et tambours d'Afrique</u>', which translates as 'Burkina Faso — Balafons and African drums' (the main language of the country is <u>French</u>, though the lyrics of <u>Yiri</u> are in an <u>African dialect</u> native to Burkina Faso).

Want to talk — just pick up the balafon and dial...

Make sure you know the <u>key features</u> of African music. Then have a <u>listen</u> to the set piece, and try and <u>spot</u> them in that. You'll need to be able to <u>recognise</u> them if you want to talk about them in your exam.

Koko — Yiri

Listen out for <u>call and response</u> in this piece — it's a key feature of sub-Saharan African music.

Yiri starts with a Solo Balafon

1) The <u>opening</u> of *Yiri* has just <u>one balafon</u> playing. When the <u>keys</u> of the balafon are hit, they produce a very <u>short</u> note. To get the <u>longer</u> notes you hear in this piece, the player has to hit the same notes <u>over and over again</u> very quickly (a bit like the way <u>steel drums</u> are played, almost a <u>roll</u>).

2) The <u>second</u> balafon <u>joins in</u> after the introduction. It's <u>pitched</u> a bit <u>lower</u> than the first.

3) The two balafons play <u>throughout</u> the rest of the piece. They're playing <u>polyrhythms</u> (see p. 64), and are <u>independent</u> of each other for most of the piece. Lots of what they play is <u>improvised</u> around the original <u>theme</u>.

4) They sometimes play in <u>heterophony</u> (see p. 65) — they're playing the <u>same melody</u> but at <u>different pitches</u>, e.g. bars 10-13.

5) The balafons either <u>complement</u> the <u>vocal</u> line or <u>boost</u> the <u>drum</u> part.

The Drums all play the Same Rhythm

1) When the <u>drums</u> come in, they all play the <u>same rhythm</u>. It's <u>repeated</u> all the way through the piece — it's an <u>ostinato</u>.

2) The drums are at <u>different pitches</u> (the <u>smaller</u> drums are <u>higher</u> than the bigger ones). The drummers can get different <u>sounds</u> from the drums by changing the <u>way</u> they <u>hit</u> them — they can hit them with <u>beaters</u> or with their <u>hands</u>.

3) The rhythm <u>changes</u> very slightly at the end of the piece and there are moments of <u>silence</u> — this <u>signals</u> to the others that the piece is about to finish.

4) At the end of *Yiri*, all the other instruments stop, except for the <u>bell</u>, which plays a final 'ting' .

The Vocal parts Change

1) The first time you hear the singers, they're singing in <u>unison</u>. The tune is quite <u>repetitive</u>.

2) Later in the piece, they use <u>call and response</u>. A <u>soloist</u> sings a phrase (the <u>call</u>) and the other singers sing the <u>response</u> in <u>unison</u>.

3) The call is fairly <u>long</u> — much longer than the response. The soloist holds some of the notes on for quite a <u>few bars</u>.

4) Towards the end of the piece, the voices sing in <u>unison</u> again.

The Timbre and Texture Build Up during the piece

1) The <u>timbre</u> (<u>tone colour</u>) is <u>developed</u> throughout the piece. It starts off with a <u>single balafon</u>, then changes slightly when the <u>second</u> is added. The <u>drums</u> change it a bit more, then the two <u>different types</u> of <u>vocals</u> (<u>unison</u> and <u>call and response</u>) produce two <u>new</u> timbres.

2) The <u>texture</u> is very <u>simple</u> to begin with, but it <u>builds up</u> too.

3) *Yiri* is <u>polyphonic</u> — the different parts weave in and out of each other. There are at least <u>four</u> <u>distinct parts</u> — <u>two balafons</u>, the <u>drums</u> and the <u>singers</u>, and they're all <u>independent</u> of each other.

A nice cup of Koko before bed...

The easiest way to learn about this piece is to look at each section of the group <u>separately</u>. Concentrate on the <u>balafon</u> parts, then listen to the <u>drums</u>, then finally focus on the <u>vocal</u> parts.

Revision Summary

Congratulations — you've made it to the end of the book. There's just one more trifling (mmm, trifle) little revision summary to go, then it's over. Unless of course there are any bits you want to have another look at. Make sure you can answer all the questions on this page before you even think about stopping though.

1) Name four popular instruments used in British folk music.
2) Name the four main types of British folk music.
3) What type of scales do folk tunes tend to use?
4) Where does Celtic music come from?
5) Name five traditional instruments and three more modern instruments played by Capercaillie.
6) Describe the process of 'waulking'.
7) What time signature is *Skye Waulking Song* in?
8) Describe three differences between the two sections of *Skye Waulking Song*.
9) What are vocables?
10) Where do the words of *Skye Waulking Song* come from?
11) What is a raga?
12) Name five instruments used in Indian Classical Music.
13) What do *tivra* and *komal* mean?
14) What instrument plays the rhythm in Indian Classical Music? What's the rhythm called?
15) What does the tambura do?
16) Describe the four different sections of a raga.
17) When is the Rag Desh supposed to be played?
18) What feelings is the Rag Desh supposed to inspire?
19) Write out the raga used for the Rag Desh.
20) Which sections of a raga do you hear in 'Priyagitah'?
21) Name the two melodic instruments played in 'Priyagitah'.
22) How many beats are there in a *rupak* tala? How many are there in an *ektal* tala?
23) What instrument does Anoushka Shankar play in Rag Desh?
24) Describe the structure of the Rag Desh from 'Live at the Carnegie Hall'.
25) Which two talas are used in this Rag Desh? How many beats do they have?
26) Name two different vocal techniques the singer uses in 'Mewar Re Mira'.
27) What is the name of the last section of this Rag Desh?
28) How is African drum music passed down?
29) Name three different types of African drum.
30) Name three different ways that drums can be played.
31) Describe the master drummer's job.
32) Name three other African instruments (not drums).
33) What are polyrhythms? What are cross-rhythms?
34) Name four key features of sub-Saharan African music.
35) What is heterophony?
36) Where do Koko come from?
37) Give three themes of Koko's music.
38) How do you produce a long note on a balafon?
39) Describe the two different ways the singers perform in *Yiri*.
40) Describe the texture of *Yiri*.

Air Guitar

Air guitar is a relatively new musical style. It developed about 25 or so years ago, when Mr. Osbourne was more famous than his wife and spent his time biting the heads off bats.

Air Guitar uses the Same Techniques as Real Guitar

First things first. Playing air guitar is exactly the same as playing a real guitar. The only difference is there's no guitar. So, like any beginner (real) guitarist, you need to learn some basic techniques:

1) Learn how to hold your 'guitar'. Find one that matches your size, and practise holding it in the right position. Always practise this in front of a mirror.

2) Get the stance right. Your feet should be at least 60 cm apart*.
   For general posture ideas, think caveman/woman.

      * *This is only true if you're playing rock music from the 70s onwards. For example, if you were playing 50s-style rock'n'roll you would need an entirely different stance — feet together, no movement from waist down, top half of body swaying from left to right, cheesy grin...*

3) Make sure you always look like you're concentrating really really hard. This is particularly important during widdly bits.

4) Hair time. If you don't have long hair, it's very important that you pretend you do have long hair. Move the head forwards and backwards in time with the music, throwing your hair everywhere. If you're doing it properly you should soon notice your hair starting to stick to your sweaty face and get caught in your mouth and nose. Perfect this hair technique and you're well on your way.

You need to Learn the Three Classic Moves:

The 'Down-on-One-Knee' Manoeuvre is Easy

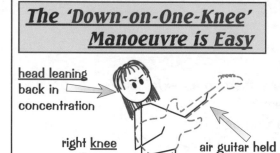

head leaning back in concentration

right knee on floor

air guitar held proudly aloft

'The Windmill' Takes a Bit More Practice...

right hand forming perfect circles

The trick is getting the circle to pass through the point where you would hit the strings (if you were playing a real guitar). This requires both technique and confidence. It's easy to look like an idiot if you mess it up.

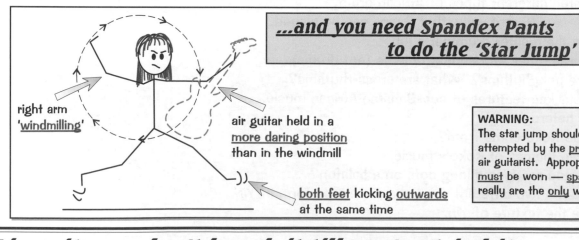

...and you need Spandex Pants to do the 'Star Jump'

right arm 'windmilling'

air guitar held in a more daring position than in the windmill

both feet kicking outwards at the same time

WARNING:
The star jump should only be attempted by the professional air guitarist. Appropriate clothing must be worn — spandex pants really are the only way to go.

Air guitar — don't knock it till you've tried it...

And finally... I'd like to finish off the page with a list of recommended tunes to practise air guitar to.
1. Sweet Child O' Mine (G'n'R)   2. Eye of the Tiger (Survivor)   3. Bohemian Rhapsody (Queen)
4. Run to the Hills (Iron Maiden)   5. Livin' on a Prayer (Bon Jovi)   6. Money for Nothing (Dire Straits)

Glossary and Index

There are so many tricky technical terms in GCSE Music, so I thought I'd be nice and give you some definitions here.

12-bar blues Style of blues with a 12-bar repeating chord pattern. **41, 44, 46**

12-tone system Schoenberg's composition system, which involves rearranging the 12 **chromatic** notes of an octave into a set order. Also known as **serialism**. **30**

A

a capella Singing with no instrumental backing. **64**

acciaccatura An **ornament** that's played as quickly as possible before the written note. **12**

action song A song in a **musical** that tells you what's going on. A bit like a **recitative**. **36**

additive melody A **minimalist** technique where you add one note or rest each time a melody is repeated, so it gets longer and longer. **31, 34**

air Another name for an **aria**. **13**

alap The first phase of a **raga** performance. **59-61**

All Blues **44-45**

alto Low female or high male voice. Sings roughly from the F below middle C to the F at the top of the treble clef stave. **13-15**

ambient Slow, chilled club dance music. **50**

anacrusis An upbeat. **54**

And the Glory of the Lord **14-15**

appoggiatura An **ornament** that clashes with the accompanying chord then resolves. **12, 38**

Area of Study 1

aria Solo vocal piece in an **opera**, **oratorio** or **cantata**. Shows the character's emotions. **9, 13, 36**

art music Music that's written down (unlike **folk music**). **27**

atonal Music that's not written in any key. **27-29**

B

balafon West African xylophone. **64-66**

ballad A song that tells a story. **54**

bandish A song that forms the final phase of a **raga** performance. Known as **gat** if it's played only on instruments (without voice). **59, 61**

bansuri A bamboo flute used in **Indian Classical Music**. **57, 60-61**

Baroque Musical style of the 17th and early 18th centuries. It has lots of contrasts in dynamics and **ornamentation**. **8-13**

bass Low male voice that can sing from about the F below the bass clef to the E above middle C. **13-15**

basso continuo A continuous bass part in **Baroque** music, often played on the **harpsichord**. **8, 14**

bebop A type of **jazz** characterised by complex harmonies and fast, syncopated rhythms. **42, 44**

big band A band that plays **jazz** and **swing music**. **42-43**

binary form Type of music in two distinct sections. **8-9**

block chord Chord played by sounding all the notes at once. **17**

blue notes Flattened 3rds, 7ths and sometimes 5ths of a **major** scale. **40, 43**

blues Style of 20th century music from America with a distinctive scale and **swung rhythms**. **40-42**

blues scale A **major** scale with a flattened 3rd and 7th (and sometimes 5th). **40**

bodhrán An Irish framed drum used in **Celtic folk music**. **55**

bouzouki A string instrument a bit like a mandolin. Played in **Celtic folk music**. **55-56**

breakbeats Electronic music that has **syncopation** or **polyrhythms**. **50**

bridge section A bit of music that bridges a gap between sections. **19, 21, 52**

Broadway A famous theatre street in New York. **35**

broken chord Chord that's played as a series of notes. **17, 23, 47**

Burkina Faso A country in Western Africa and homeland of **Koko**. **62, 65**

C

cadence Pair of chords used to finish off a phrase. **15, 18, 25**

cadenza Section of a piece where a soloist can really show off. **19, 23**

call and response A short melody (the call) followed by an answering phrase (the response). **40, 43, 63-66**

canon Where the same tune is played by two or more parts, each starting before the previous part has finished. Also called a round. **15, 34**

cantata Vocal piece made up of 2 or 3 **arias**, separated by **recitatives**. **13**

Capercaillie **55-56**

Celtic folk music Western European **folk music** particularly popular in Scotland and Ireland. **55-56**

Chopin **24-25**

choral music Music written for choirs. **13**

chorale A hymn. **13**

chorus Piece in an **opera**, **oratorio** or **cantata** sung by the chorus (choir). **13-15**

chorus number A piece in a **musical** sung by the whole cast. Similar to a **chorus** in **opera**. **36**

chromatics Notes that don't belong to the main scale of a melody. **21, 27**

Classical Either any music that's not pop (or jazz, folk, hip-hop etc.) or the period of western classical music from about 1750-1820. **8-12, 16-21**

cluster chords Chords made up of notes that are really close together. **30**

coda A bit at the end of a piece that's different to the rest of it and finishes it off nicely. **19, 21, 24**

codetta A mini **coda**, used to finish off a section of a piece. **21**

comping Chords played on the guitar or piano underneath an **improvised** solo. **43**

complement The six semitones not used in a **hexachord**. **29**

composition **1, 3-6**

concept album An album where all the tracks are linked by a theme. **46**

concerto A piece for soloist and orchestra, usually in three movements. **18**

contrast **5-6**

coursework 1

cross-rhythms Two or more rhythms that don't fit together are played at the same time. **38, 64-65**

Cubase A piece of software used as a sequencer. **48, 52**

D

delay Adds echoes to music. **49**

development The middle section in **sonata form** where ideas are developed. **19, 21**

diatonic Notes that belong to the main key of the piece. **17, 36**

dissonance Chords with clashing notes. **27, 29**

distortion An effect used on an electric guitar to distort notes. **46-47**

Dixieland jazz Music that was a mix of brass band marches, **ragtime** and **blues** that came from New Orleans at the start of the 20th century. **42**

djembe Single-headed African drum played with the hands. **62, 65**

donno African drum, also known as a **talking drum**. **62, 65**

Glossary and Index

Glossary and Index

Glossary and Index